Learning Matters:

Helping Students Increase Their Learning Power by Learning About Learning

By Maggie Hoody

A TiP Learning Publication

Cover design by Kathrine Gutkovskiy.

Cover image from *The Thing Lou Couldn't Do* written and illustrated by Ashley Spires is used by permission of Kids Can Press Ltd., Toronto, Canada. Illustrations © 2017 Ashley Spires

Cover image from *Jabari Jumps* written and illustrated by Gaia Cornwall is used by permission of Candlewick Press, Somerville, Massachusetts.

Cover image from *Andres and His Rubik's Cube Madness* written by Andrea Alvarez is used by permission of Andrea Alvarez.

ISBN: 978-1-7371091-0-5

TiP Learning
www.tiplearning.com

Contents

Time Recommendation

The module is designed to take place once or twice a week across the first six weeks of a school year. Each lesson will likely require 30 – 60 minutes. The module is also a good fit for the beginning of a new quarter, semester, or course.

About TiP Learning

The name TiP Learning has roots in theory into practice (TiP) pedagogy and reflects the idea that all educational endeavors are based on theories of how people acquire new knowledge and abilities. Ongoing research across multiple disciplines offers evidence-based insight on how learning happens and which instructional strategies may work best for a particular learning goal. While we may not always explicitly identify the theories of learning at play in our instructional practice, when we do strategically align learning goals with theories of learning we increase learning power and "TiP" towards deeper, more coherent learning that lasts.

TiP Learning specializes in design and facilitation of curriculum that applies evidence-based research to classroom instruction across K – 12 and higher education. Each lesson plan explicitly identifies the instructional strateg(ies) utilized. Within each TiP Learning publication, the scholarship that supports the curricular design is identified in narrative and bibliographic form.

Acknowledgments

There are many who have contributed to the design and creation of this book. First and foremost, I am grateful to all of the students and teachers I have had the privilege to work with throughout the arc of my education and career in education.

In addition, I am grateful to the following:

Chris Bradbeer and the Stonefields School in Auckland, New Zealand for generously sharing their approach to theory to practice teaching and learning. In particular, for sharing the model they designed for helping learners develop an understanding of learner qualities.

James Nottingham for sharing the concept of the Learning Pit and allowing its inclusion in this text.

Teachers at Lincoln K – 8 Choice School in Rochester, Minnesota for their participation in an action research project through InSciEd Out that focused on the role of feedback on student learning.

Teacher candidates at Winona State University in Rochester, Minnesota for celebrating the concept of the learning zone despite the frustration that sometimes accompanied it.

Kathrine Gutkovskiy for collaborating to create the cover illustrations.

Meg Bowman and Class Dojo for allowing me to include links to the Class Dojo videos and discussion prompts.

Gaia Cornwall and Candlewick Press for allowing me to include the image of *Jabari Jumps*.

Andrea Alvarez for allowing me to include the image of *Andres and His Rubik's Cube Madness*.

Ashley Spires and Kids Can Press for allowing me to include the image of *The Thing Lou Couldn't Do*.

Tom Peacock for reminding me that writing is teaching, too.

Tom Gniadek for reminding me that it's possible to parent and publish.

Dear Reader,

Whether your aim is to grow students' capacities as readers, mathematicians, scientists, soccer players, musicians, artists or friends, one of the most important steps we can take as educators is to help children learn about learning. This enables students of all ages to take a more active role in their development across all disciplines within and beyond classrooms.

This book was written using a theory-into-practice approach to teaching and learning. Each section begins with a brief overview of the theory that guides the lessons that follow. Paying attention to how theory informs practice helps ensure we reach the goals we are aiming for when planning and facilitating instruction.

The lesson plans within this book include detailed teacher-talk (*denoted by italicized text*) to provide insight on how each session might be facilitated in a classroom. The aim was not to script the lessons verbatim, but rather to offer a framework that could be sculpted to fit the context of each unique classroom community.

The lessons are written in a manner that can be adapted across grades K – 8. When possible, lessons have been differentiated to honor the range of developmental abilities present within primary, intermediate, and middle level classrooms.

The lessons are arranged into three distinct but interrelated phases of learning about learning:
1. The Nature of Learning
2. Learner Qualities
3. Planning & Monitoring a Learning Journey

Any set of these lessons could be facilitated independent from the others. I invite you to join the learning about learning journey wherever it best fits the needs of your students.

Appendices A – C contain materials to support implementation of the lessons in your classroom. Documents denoted with a ✎ within Appendices A and B may be reproduced for student use. An electronic copy of these documents is available at https://www.tiplearning.com/free-resources.

At the time of publication, design and development of Learning Tool Cards to accompany students' developing metacognition of learning tools is in progress. Check the TiP Learning website (www.tiplearning.com) for updates and availability.

Finally, if you have questions or concerns about any of the content in this book please contact me at maggie@tiplearning.com.

Learning Intention: I understand what learning is and how to use my awareness of the learning process to grow my knowledge and abilities.

	Success Criteria
Lesson 1: **What is Learning?**	❑ I can reflect on a time I learned something and explain how I knew I was learning. ❑ I can describe the difference between learning and practicing.
Lesson 2: **Where Does Learning Come From?**	❑ I can respond to the question "Where does learning come from?" based on my own experience and storybook characters' experiences.
Lesson 3: **The Learning Pit**	❑ I can use the Learning Pit to map and describe my journey as a learner.
Lesson 4a - c: **Jabari Jumps, The Thing Lou Couldn't Do, or Andres and His Rubik's Cube Madness**	❑ I can use the Learning Pit to map and describe a storybook character's journey as a learner.
Lesson 5: **Learner Qualities**	❑ I can identify qualities of a strong learner. ❑ I can use a progression to grow the "Be Determined" quality.
Lesson 6: **Learner Qualities**	❑ I can identify qualities of a strong learner. ❑ I can use a progression to grow the "Connect" quality.
Lesson 7: **Setting Learner Goals**	❑ I can identify two learning goals I have this _____ (enter time duration here, i.e. week, month, quarter, trimester, semester). ❑ I can use the learning goal template to develop a plan to help me reach the learning goal I have identified.
Lesson 8: **Learning Tools**	❑ I can identify a learning tool, explain its purpose, and describe how to use it. ❑ I can select and use learning tools as part of a learning journey.
Lesson 9: **Learning Talks**	❑ I can participate in a Learning Talk to provide helpful feedback to another learner. ❑ I can use feedback from a Learning Talk to advance my progress toward a learning goal.
Lesson 10: **Progress Monitoring**	❑ I can use the progress monitoring template to assess my progress toward a learning goal.
Lesson 11: **Essential Questions Revisited**	❑ I can reflect on what I've learned about learning.

Materials Needed

Lesson 1: **What is Learning?**	❑ Copies of Learning Reflection recording page (1 per student) ❑ Copies of Essential Question prompts (1 per student) ❑ Chart Paper or SMART Board ❑ Markers ❑ Poster-sized copy of Essential Questions
Lesson 2: **Where Does** **Learning Come** **From?**	❑ Copies of essential questions displayed on wall ❑ Sticky notes (~3 per student) ❑ Chart paper ❑ Copies of Look, Think, Write exit slip (1 per student) ❑ Children's literature that features sources of learning (see list of possibilities on page 20)
Lesson 3: **The Learning Pit**	❑ Copies of Learning Pit diagram (1 per student) ❑ Copies of Learning Pit diagram with blank spaces for application task (1 per student) ❑ Poster-size version of Learning Pit (optional) ❑ Lesson 3 exit slip (1 per student)
Lesson 4a: **Jabari Jumps** **Lesson 4b:** **The Thing Lou** **Couldn't Do** **Lesson 4c:** **Andres and His** **Rubik's Cube** **Madness**	❑ Copy of *Jabari Jumps* by Gaia Cornwall, ❑ Copy of *The Thing Lou Couldn't Do* by Ashley Spires. OR ❑ Copy of *Andres and His Rubik's Cube Madness* by Andrea Alvarez ❑ Word cloud template (2 per student) ❑ Empty copy of The Learning Pit (poster-size) ❑ Photo of each student (optional)
Lesson 5: **Learner Qualities** **"Be Determined"**	❑ Smart Board for viewing videos ❑ Cover images (Appendix page 100); 1 per student OR projection ❑ "Be Determined" poster ❑ "Be Determined" progression (1 per student) ❑ "Be Determined" exit slip (1 per student)
Lesson 6: **Learner Qualities** **"Make** **Connections"**	❑ Smart Board for viewing videos ❑ Making Connections: What is a neuron? (1 per student) ❑ Additional source of information about neurons* (see list at end of lesson plan for possibilities) ❑ "Connect" poster ❑ "Connect" progression (1 copy per student)

Lesson 7: Setting Learning Goals	❑ Sample standards/benchmarks. ❑ Smart Board ❑ Goal Setting Template (1 copy per student) ❑ Anchor chart copy of Goal Setting Template ❑ Differentiated materials for sample lesson plans (see next page) K-1: ❑ Copy of the book "Mrs. Wishy Washy" ❑ Farm Workmat (1 per student) ❑ Full copy of Sample K – 1 content-based lesson plan (Appendix B) 2-3: ❑ Watch, Write, Wonder recording page (1 per student) ❑ Small tanks ❑ Tadpoles (1 per small group for ½ of class) ❑ Frogs (1 per small group for ½ of class) ❑ Full copy of sample grades 2– 3 content-based lesson plan (Appendix B) 4-6: ❑ Natural Resources Jigsaw Task Card (1 per student) ❑ Nature Resources Jigsaw Poster Requirements (1 per student) ❑ Nature Resources Jigsaw Exchange of Expertise (1 per student) ❑ "Our Natural Resources" by Jennifer Prior (available on Epic books) ❑ Full copy of grades 4 – 6 content-based lesson plan (Appendix B)
Lesson 8: Learning Tools	❑ Think-Write-Share Template (1 per student) ❑ Learning Tool Template (or Learning Tool Cards) ❑ Hammer ❑ Potato Peeler ❑ Differentiated Materials by Grade Level (see Appendix B)
Lesson 9: Learning Talks	❑ Think-Write-Share recording page ❑ Role Cards (1 set per group) ❑ Learning Talk Protocol Presenter Guide (1 per presenter) ❑ Learning Talk Protocol Reviewer Guide (1 per reviewer)
Lesson 10: Monitoring Learning Progress	❑ Goal-setting forms (completed in lesson 6) ❑ Learner quality rubrics ❑ Evidence of learning (See Saw, videos, etc.)
Lesson 11: Essential Questions Revisited	❑ Copies of Essential Question prompts (1 per student) ❑ Original Essential Question recording pages (from Lesson 1) ❑ Final Reflection

Note: All recording pages can be found in Appendices A and B.

Chapter 1: Introduction – The Nature of Learning

The odds are good that if you are reading this book, you agree with the title: **Learning Matters**. But what *is* learning? How do we do know if students are learning? How do *students* know if they are learning? And perhaps most important of all, how do we help students learn about learning?

An interesting phenomenon occurs in schools when students become familiar with completing activities that do not challenge them to engage with complex tasks: They can forget how to learn. Students become accustomed to schoolwork being more practice-based and less learning-based. They feel capable completing worksheets, responding to closed questions on an iPad, or performing simple tasks. Then, when faced with scenarios that require more complex learning, helpless mindsets take hold.

I've seen this phenomenon in first grade classrooms as often as in undergraduate and graduate-level classrooms. Students shut down, display anger or frustration, and often feel lost when they are challenged to complete a task that requires real learning. The first grader who cannot (yet) blend three sounds to form a word, the seventh grader who cannot (yet) solve a linear equation, the aspiring teacher candidate who cannot (yet) differentiate a reading lesson across four guided reading levels – each is hampered by frustration and a general sense of despair. If left unchecked, the helplessness impacts the student's response to the present learning opportunity and creeps into to the psyche of future learning as well. As Dweck (2000) would say, helpless mindsets take root. *"I'm just not* good at this." *"I've never been a math person." "Maybe teaching isn't for me."*

Encouraging students to identify mindsets assists them in understanding their thoughts about intelligence (Dweck, 2000). Helping students understand learning equips them with tools to manage their mindsets while on a learning journey. This book was written to help teachers help students learning about learning and – as a result – increase their learning power within and beyond classrooms.

What is learning?

I had been a teacher for five years before I explicitly examined the nature of learning. As a graduate student in experiential education, I returned to the classroom as a learner and opted to take a graduate-level ceramics course having never studied ceramics before. I was eager to learn a new skill and had fanciful visions of a houseful of self-made ceramic wares. My enthusiasm for the grand adventure quickly evolved into a profound case of stress and anxiety. No matter how hard I tried, I could not get the clay to behave the way my mind envisioned, the way my instructor advised, or the way the students around me seemed to effortlessly accomplish. The frustration was so intense that I contemplated dropping the course.

While working in the ceramics studio one day it occurred to me that stress was inhibiting my ability to learn. Worse yet, I realized that the way I was feeling about clay and ceramic sculpture was likely similar to the way many of my middle school students felt about solving linear equations, writing a scientific lab report, or some other aspect of learning I had asked them to engage in. I could hear echoes of my teacher-voice reassuring students, *"You can do it. Don't be stressed."* Suddenly, that advice seemed woefully misguided.

My experience in the ceramics studio challenged me to recognize that learning something new is profoundly different than practicing something one is already familiar with. Learning something new is inherently perplexing at some point in the process. Look no further than a baby learning to walk or a child navigating a set of monkey bars for the first time to see evidence of this in action. Learning requires risk, tenacity, and resilience, among other attributes. When we purposefully expose and carefully examine the qualities of learning, we empower learners to see challenge in the process rather than shortcomings in themselves.

How do I know when I'm learning?

When I returned to teaching the following year, I brought a clearer sense of learning awareness with me. My students and I worked together to identify when we were practicing something reasonably familiar to them and when we hit what we came to call "the learning zone". Similar to Vygotsky's *Zone of Proximal Development* (1978) or Dewey's *Pattern of Inquiry* (1938), "the learning zone" identified the moment when we left familiar terrain and confronted skills, content, or procedures the students were otherwise unfamiliar with. With this explicit awareness in place, students were better able to welcome uncertainty, support one another through frustration, and celebrate accomplishments when learning happened.

Years later I came upon a model developed by James Nottingham commonly referred to as the "Learning Pit" (Nottingham, 2007; 2010; 2017). In short, Nottingham created a child-friendly way to explain *Vygotsky's Zone of Proximal Development* (1978) so that he could encourage his students to step out of their comfort zone, take more intellectual risks, and engage in collaborative thinking. The Learning Pit has since become a widely utilized tool to help educators know how, when and why to challenge students appropriately; to build the social and emotional learning of students by giving them additional opportunities to solve problems together; and to place concepts at the heart of the learning journey.

Nottingham's model is not all that different from John Dewey's *Pattern of Inquiry* (1938). Dewey, considered by many to be the father of experiential education, also believed that learning follows a predictable pattern. In his model, a person begins with a state of perplexity about a particular topic, concept, or question. From there, s/he clarifies the problem, develops an hypothesis, tests the hypothesis, and reflects on the outcome. Knowledge acquired throughout the inquiry cycle leads a learner toward a depth of understanding that enables him/her to ask more complex questions about the topic or concept of focus. In this sense, learning begets learning.

Dewey's, Vygotsky's, and Nottingham's models all point toward a common theme —> Learning is hard work. This brings us to another challenge of teaching and learning: As teachers it is often easy for us to forget what it feels like to really learn something new. A model of schooling in which educators address the same content and concepts year after year can exacerbate this tendency. The more familiar we become with ideas at our grade level, the less patience we may have for learners as they work to negotiate the challenges of learning to add with regrouping, write a topic sentence, or negotiate peer dynamics on the playground. We forget how challenging it really is to learn these skills for the first time.

Perhaps one of the most important steps we can take as educators is to challenge ourselves to learn something new every year; *really new*, as in completely outside our wheelhouse. For me, this challenge has led to a ceramics studio, a marathon training program, and a rowing club on the shores of Lake Superior (to name a few). Each time, despite everything I knew about mindsets and the pattern of inquiry, I repeatedly found myself frustrated and stuck. I wanted to drop out of the ceramics class, convinced the clay could sense my incompetence. I wished I had only signed up for the half-marathon; fewer miles, same free food at the end. I was certain the 8-person shell would crush my vertebrae and that my arms would never acquire the strength, skill, and stamina necessary to row in sync with the rest of my team. Each time I subjected myself to real learning, I was reminded of the visceral response our minds and bodies have to the difficulties we encounter throughout the learning process. Sometimes we simply have to shut down, regroup, and try again another day. Other times, a deep breath and short break are sufficient fuel for another try. Most importantly, when we finally get it — when we finally *learn* — the pride and sense of accomplishment are second to none.

Each time we have the experience of being a student, we strengthen our capacity as teachers. Revisiting learning as students offers us the opportunity to better understand the nature and dynamics of the learning process. This level of insight is equally valuable to K – 8 students. If we really want students to learn – no matter what the skill or setting – one of the most important steps we can take with them is to explore the nature of learning: *What is learning? How do I know when I'm learning? What are the qualities of strong learners? How do I plan and monitor a learning journey?*

The pages that follow include a series of ten lessons to guide this exploration. Lessons examine where learning comes from, the concept of the "Learning Pit," qualities of strong learners, and how to plan and monitor a learning journey. This guide aims to develop students' awareness around the nature of learning and scaffold how they can use what they know about learning to grow their skills and abilities across disciplines within and beyond classrooms.

Appendices A and B include copies of student-documents to support the module.

Electronic copies of these documents can also be found on Maggie's website: www.tiplearning.com

Lessons-At-A-Glance

Lesson 1: What is Learning?

This introductory lesson challenges students to think about the nature of learning.

Lesson 2: Where Does Learning Come From?

This lesson invites students to think about the variety of sources that learning come from.

Lesson 3: The Learning Zone/The Learning Pit

This lesson introduces students to the concept of the Learning Pit and challenges them to use the Learning Pit as a map for their own learning journeys.

Lesson 4a: Jabari Jumps

This lesson extends students' understanding of the Learning Pit by challenging them to map a storybook character's learning experience onto the Learning Pit map.

Lesson 4b: The Thing Lou Couldn't Do

This lesson extends students' understanding of the Learning Pit by challenging them to map a storybook character's learning experience onto the Learning Pit map.

Lesson 4c: Andres and His Rubik's Cube Madness

This lesson extends students' understanding of the Learning Pit by challenging them to map a storybook character's learning experience onto the Learning Pit map.

Lesson 5: Learner Qualities

This lesson introduces students to the idea of learner qualities: attributes that lead to strong learning.

Lesson 6: Learner Qualities

This lesson continues the exploration of learner qualities.

Lesson 7: Setting Learning Goals

This lesson challenges students to create and manage a learning goal for themselves.

(continued on next page)

Lesson 8: Learning Tools

This lesson introduces students to the concept of learning tools; strategies that can be used to promote learning.

Lesson 9: Learning Talks

This lesson guides students through the process of providing constructive feedback on one another's learning goals.

Lesson 10: Monitoring Learning Progress

This lesson challenges students to reflect on the progress they've made around a specific learning goal and use evidence to support their evaluation.

Lesson 11: Essential Questions Revisited

This lesson challenges students to respond to the essential questions again and reflect on how their understanding of learning has evolved since Lesson 1.

Chapter Two: "The Nature of Learning" Lessons

Lesson 1: What is Learning?	
Overview	This lesson challenges students to think about the nature of learning.
Learning Intention	I understand what learning is and how to use my awareness of the learning process to grow my knowledge and abilities.
Success Criteria	Note: Within the lesson plans in the book, the success criteria listed in ***bold italicized font*** reflect the focus of each lesson. ❑ ***I can reflect on a time I learned something new and explain how I knew I was learning.*** ❑ ***I can describe the difference between learning and practicing.*** ❑ I can respond to the question "Where does learning come from?" based on my own experience and storybook characters' experiences. ❑ I can use the Learning Pit to map and describe my journey as a learner. ❑ I can use the Learning Pit to map and describe a storybook character's journey as a learner. ❑ I can identify qualities of a strong learner. ❑ I understand how to use a progression to grow learner qualities. ❑ I can list learning goals I have this _____ (enter time duration here, i.e. week, month, quarter, trimester, semester). ❑ I can use the learning goal template to develop a plan to help me reach the learning goal I have identified. ❑ I can identify a learning tool, explain its purpose, and describe how to use it. ❑ I can select and use learning tools as part of a learning journey. ❑ I can participate in a Learning Talk to provide helpful feedback to another learner. ❑ I can use feedback from a Learning Talk to advance my progress toward a learning goal. ❑ I can use the progress monitoring template to assess my progress toward a learning goal.
Materials	❑ Copies Learning Reflection recording page (1 per student) ❑ Copies of Essential Question prompts (1 per student) ❑ Chart Paper or SMART Board ❑ Markers ❑ Poster-sized copy of Essential Questions

Essential Questions	1. What is learning?
	2. How do I know when I'm learning?
	3. What makes a strong learner?
	4. How do I plan and monitor a learning journey?
Instructional Strategies	• Think-Pair-Share
	• Definitional Investigation
	• Creating Cognitive Conflict
	• Learning Wall (Audit Trail)
Instructional Plan	**Part I: Introduction to the Concept of Learning**
	Good Morning! Today we are going to begin an investigation about learning. We gather here each and every day of the week for the purpose of learning, but what exactly is learning? How do you know when you are learning? What can get in the way of learning? What makes a strong learner?
	These are just some of the questions we will reflect on. To get us started, I want you to spend 5 minutes generating a list of everything you learned over the summer (or a previous period of time; i.e. last quarter, last month).
	Distribute Learning Reflection recording pages (1 per student). Allow students 5 minutes to generate a list of things they learned over the summer.
	Next, we're going to focus in on one of the ideas you included on your list. Take a moment to think about which idea you'd like to share with another classmate and, when you're ready, circle that idea on your paper.
	Prompt 1
	Now, with your partner, take turns sharing a response to the following prompt:
	➢ Last summer I learned _____.
	Allow groups of two to share their responses to the prompt. Then, facilitate a whole class discussion.
	Let's hear from some of the groups.
	What was something you learned this past summer?

Record all ideas on chart paper, SMART Board, or anchor chart.

Next, I want you think about <u>how you knew you were learning</u>. In the righthand column of your recording page, use words and/or pictures to explain how you knew you were learning.

Prompt 2
  ➢ *I knew I was learning because* _____.

Transition to whole group discussion, "Let's hear from some of the groups"

How did you know you were learning?

Record all ideas on SMART Board or anchor chart.

I learned...	I knew I was learning because...
How to ride a bike	I could finally ride the bike without falling.
How to swim the crawl stroke	I passed the swim test.
How to play the game cribbage	I could play the game with my uncles and I didn't need any help.
...	...

As you discuss these ideas, work to create a sense of cognitive conflict by challenging different ideas. Possible paths to follow include:

  ➢ *Were you <u>learning</u>, or were you <u>practicing</u> something you'd already learned? Is there a difference? Why or why not?*
  ➢ *How do you know when you're learning something?*
  ➢ *Did the learning feel good, or not? Why or why not?*
  ➢ *Can **you** tell when you're learning something, or does someone else have to be the judge of that?*

As I mentioned earlier, we are going to spend time this year thinking very deliberately about learning and what makes a strong learner. To begin that journey, I want you to take the rest of our time this morning to reflect on the following questions:

  ➢ What is learning?
  ➢ How do I know when I'm learning?
  ➢ What makes a strong learner?
  ➢ How do I plan and monitor a learning journey?

	This step will document the beginning of our learning about learning journey. Write or draw your response to each of the four questions. This will capture your thinking about learning <u>now</u> so we can compare it to our thinking <u>later</u> to see how our ideas have grown or changed.
	
	Task (pre-assessment)
	Working independently, write and/or draw a response to each question.
	
	   ➤ ***What is learning?***
	   ➤ ***How do I know when I'm learning?***
	   ➤ ***What makes a strong learner?***
	   ➤ ***How do I plan and monitor a learning journey?***
	Allow students 10 minutes (or more) to generate responses to the essential questions listed above. As they finish, have them turn their work in. When everyone has finished, close the lesson as follows.
	
	Closure
	Over the course of the next several weeks we will continue to explore the nature of learning. Today represents the beginning of that journey. We will revisit these questions throughout the days and weeks to come. Our goal is to build a deeper understanding of what it means to be and become a strong learner.

Assessment	Review (and save) student responses to pre-assessment (task 3) above. Also, add questions "What is learning?" and "How do I know when I'm learning?" to a learning wall to begin documentation of the learning journey. See Appendix C for an explanation of the Audit Trail (Harste & Vasquez, 1998; Vasquez, 2003; 2008). What is learning? How do I know when I'm learning?
Special Note(s)	While this lesson is written in a manner that asks students to reflect on learning completed over the summer, a different duration of time would work as well. Appendix A includes reflection templates for learning last week, last month, last quarter, and more.

Lesson 2: Where Does Learning Come From?	
Overview	This lesson invites students to think about the variety of sources that learning come from.
Learning Intention	I understand what learning is and how to use my awareness of the learning process to grow my knowledge and abilities.
Success Criteria	❑ I can reflect on a time I learned something new and explain how I knew I was learning. ❑ I can describe the difference between learning and practicing. ❑ ***I can respond to the question "Where does learning come from?" based on my own experience and storybook characters' experiences.*** ❑ I can use the Learning Pit to map and describe my journey as a learner. ❑ I can use the Learning Pit to map and describe a storybook character's journey as a learner. ❑ I can identify qualities of a strong learner. ❑ I understand how to use a progression to grow learner qualities. ❑ I can list learning goals I have this _____ (enter time duration here, i.e. week, month, quarter, trimester, semester). ❑ I can use the learning goal template to develop a plan to help me reach the learning goal I have identified. ❑ I can identify a learning tool, explain its purpose, and describe how to use it. ❑ I can select and use learning tools as part of a learning journey. ❑ I can participate in a Learning Talk to provide helpful feedback to another learner. ❑ I can use feedback from a Learning Talk to advance my progress toward a learning goal. ❑ I can use the progress monitoring template to assess my progress toward a learning goal.
Materials	❑ Copies of essential questions displayed on wall ❑ Sticky notes (~3 per student) ❑ Chart paper ❑ Copies of Look, Think, Write exit slip (1 per student) ❑ Children's literature that features sources of learning (see list of possibilities on page 20)
Essential Questions	1. What is learning? 2. How do I know when I'm learning? 3. What makes a strong learner? 4. How do I plan and monitor a learning journey?

Instructional Strategies	<ul><li>Learning Wall (Audit Trail)</li><li>Reflection</li><li>Co-Constructed Anchor Chart</li><li>Read-Aloud</li></ul>
Instructional Plan	**Introduction** *Today we're going to continue on our journey "Learning About Learning". Last week we spent time thinking about things you learned this past summer and how you knew you were learning.* Point to the questions "What is learning?" and "How do I know if I'm learning?" on the learning wall. *Take a minute to think back to that discussion. How did we respond to those questions? Be ready to share with your turn-and-talk partner.* Allow dyads to share. *Today we are going to challenge ourselves to think about the question, "Where does learning come from?"* Add "Where does learning come from?" question to the learning wall. **Reflection Prompt 1** ➤ **Where does learning come from?** *Take a moment to think about that question. Record the ideas you have on sticky notes. Put one idea per sticky note. Be ready to share the ideas that come to your mind with your turn-and-talk partner.*

When students are ready, prompt them to share ideas with their turn-and-talk partner. Then, gather ideas as a whole class. Co-construct an anchor chart using the sticky notes students have recorded their ideas on. Likely responses include, *"From school,"* *"From my brain,"* and *"From books."*

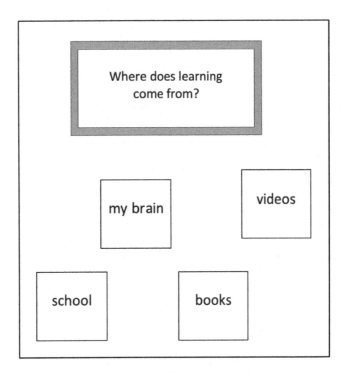

Next, work to create a bit of cognitive disequilibrium by stating, *We come to school every day and we often think of schools as <u>the</u> place of learning, but is school the only source of learning, or not?*

Reflection Prompt 2
> ➤ *Is school the only source of learning, or not?*

(allow students to think about this briefly)

To get us started, I have some questions for you to think about:
1. How did you learn how to tie your shoes?
2. How did you learn to talk?
3. How did you learn to ride a bike? How did you even know what a bike is or what it's for?
4. How did you learn how to play (enter game name here; i.e. "Slap Jack," "Candyland," "Sorry")?
5. How did you learn to read a book?
6. How did you learn to pump on a swing?

Teaching Notes:

1. It will be most powerful if you can build these questions with the context of your specific learners in mind. Reflect upon the interests, hobbies, and skills they possess and populate the question list above with that context in mind. In addition, invite students to build out the list, adding questions based on their own experience.

2. Create an anchor chart to organize thinking for this task.

What I learned...	Where the learning came from...
How to tie my shoes	My mom
How to ride a bike	My sister and my dad
How to play Slapjack	My uncle and my grandpa
How to read a book	My mom and my teacher
How to cross the monkey bars	My neighbor
How to ice skate	My coach
How to catch a fish	At camp
How to grow carrots	
How to bake a cake	
How to make a bracelet	

Task

As we look at this list, let's think about the question: **Where does learning come from?**

How would you answer that question based on the list we've created so far?

Use "Look, Think, Write" exit slip to document student thinking at this point in time.

Closure

Schools are places designed to grow learning, but they are not the only place that learning happens. Each of you comes to school with ___ (enter # here) years of knowledge. Some of that learning you constructed at school and some of that you built other places with other people.

When we think about all of the sources learning comes from, we open our minds to new ways of building knowledge. We can use these ways at school, and we can use them in other times and places, too.

This week we will spend time reading stories about different sources learning comes from. As we read, we'll keep track of how each story would answer the question "Where does learning come from?".

If you think of other answers to the question, "Where does learning come from?" you can add one – or more – to the wall as well.

Throughout the week, facilitate read-aloud experiences using some of the books listed below. Aim to incorporate books from across the different categories of learning.

Children's books that feature learning:

Learning from family:
Do Like Kyla by Angela Johnson
Growing Up with Tamales by Gwendolyn Zepeda
Kunu's Basket by Lee DeCora Francis
Mango, Abuela, and Me by Meg Medina
When Grandpa Gives You a Toolbox by Jamie L.B. Deenihan
drawn together by Minh Lê
A Morning with Grandpa by Sylvia Liu

Learning from friends:
The Thing Lou Couldn't Do by Ashley Spires

Learning from nature:
The Raft by Jim LeMarche
Tiny, Perfect Things by M.H. Clark

(continued on next page)

	Learning from curiosity: *Papa's Mechanical Fish* by Candace Fleming *Ada Twist Scientist* by Andrea Beaty and David Roberts *On a Beam of Light* by Jennifer Berne Learning from mentors: *Trying* by Kobi Yamada At the end of the week, review the Learning Wall, create a list together that looks something like this: Learning comes from family (parents, grandparents, brothers, sisters, aunts, uncles, etc.) Learning comes from friends. Learning comes from observing others. Learning comes from trying. Learning comes from curiosity. Learning comes from nature. Learning comes from… (leave room for additional discoveries to be made)
Assessment	Review the Look, Think, Write exit slips to gain a clearer sense of students' thinking around the question "Where does learning come from?"
Special Note	The theory guiding this lesson is known as "funds of knowledge" (Vélez-Ibáñez, C. & Greenberg, J., 1992) and is based on the notion that students bring knowledge and ways of knowing from their homes and communities that can be used as a foundation for skill and concept development in schools. When educators are deliberate about honoring students' funds of knowledge in the classroom, learners are better able to make connections between home and school and demonstrate the full capacity of their understandings (Moll, L.C., Amanti, C., Neff, D., & Gonzalez, N., 1992).

Lesson 3: The Learning Pit	
Overview	This lesson introduces students to the concept of the Learning Pit and challenges them to use the Learning Pit as a map for their own learning journeys.
Learning Intention	I understand what learning is and how to use my awareness of the learning process to grow my knowledge and abilities.
Success Criteria	❑ I can reflect on a time I learned something new and explain how I knew I was learning. ❑ I can describe the difference between learning and practicing. ❑ I can respond to the question "Where does learning come from?" based on my own experience and storybook characters' experiences. ❑ ***I can use the Learning Pit to map and describe my journey as a learner.*** ❑ I can use the Learning Pit to map and describe a storybook character's journey as a learner. ❑ I can identify qualities of a strong learner. ❑ I understand how to use a progression to grow learner qualities. ❑ I can list learning goals I have this _____ (enter time duration here, i.e. week, month, quarter, trimester, semester). ❑ I can use the learning goal template to develop a plan to help me reach the learning goal I have identified. ❑ I can identify a learning tool, explain its purpose, and describe how to use it. ❑ I can select and use learning tools as part of a learning journey. ❑ I can participate in a Learning Talk to provide helpful feedback to another learner. ❑ I can use feedback from a Learning Talk to advance my progress toward a learning goal. ❑ I can use the progress monitoring template to assess my progress toward a learning goal.
Essential Questions	1. What is learning? 2. How do I know when I'm learning? 3. What makes a strong learner? 4. How do I plan and monitor a learning journey?
Materials	❑ Copies of Learning Pit diagram (1 letter-sized per student) ❑ Copies of Learning Pit diagram with blank spaces for application task (1 per student) ❑ Poster-size version of Learning Pit (optional) ❑ Lesson 3 Exit slip (1 per student)

Instructional Strategies	• Direct Instruction
	• Guided Example
	• Context-Based Application Task
	• Think-Write-Share
	• Learning Wall (Audit Trail)
Instructional Plan	**Introduction**
	Today we are going to continue our learning about learning journey. Throughout the past week(s), we spent time thinking about how you know when you're learning and where learning comes from.
	Today we are going spend some time learning about the pattern of learning. Specifically, we will:
	1. *Learn about something called the "Learning Pit"*
	2. *Learn about how our brains construct knowledge.*
	We spend a lot of time asking you to learn at school, but we don't always pause to learn about learning.
	Today we are going to do just that. By the end of the lesson you will understand:
	1. *The concept of the Learning Pit*
	2. *How the brain constructs knowledge*
	Part I: The Learning Pit
	Project image of the Learning Pit on board.
	(*For images of the Learning Pit created by James Nottingham and Challenging Learning visit https://www.challenginglearning.com/learning-pit/free-graphics/)
	To begin, I want to share an image with you that is known as the "Learning Pit."
	The idea of the Learning Pit was developed by James Nottingham, a British educator that studies learning.
	The Learning Pit suggests that there are predictable steps – or phases – that happen when you are learning something new. Nottingham believes that if you are aware of these phases you are more likely to persevere and actually learn.

Step 1: Beginning to Learn

At this stage, people tend to think things like "I wonder. I want to. I bet I can. This will be fun!"

Step 2: The Pit

At this stage, people begin to better understand the challenge of what they are attempting to do. They think things like, "This is more challenging than I expected. I'm not sure."

Sometimes though, the more they investigate something, the more complexity they unearth. This can lead to them thinking, "I can't do this. I just don't get it. I'm just not good at this."

Step 3: Building Knowledge

At this stage, people begin to make connections between their confusion and prior knowledge or experiences they've had. They think things like, "What tools could I use?," "Let's work together," and "How can I use what I know from before to make an attempt?"

Step 4: Aha! "I found it"

At this stage people feel the reward of sticking with the challenge. They think things like, "I did it! Now I'm wondering…"

Source: https://www.challenginglearning.com/learning-pit/

Task 1: Mapping Learning to the Learning Pit
To make this map come alive for us, I have a challenge for you today. I want you to…

Task: Choose something you learned over the summer and map the learning stages on your copy of the "Learning Pit" map.

First, let's try it together. We will use an example from my life. Last year, I wanted to learn (underline)enter idea here(/underline). I was super excited to learn this because (underline)enter reason here(/underline). (See example below to guide the version you create with your students.)

Guided Example: (Complete the map yourself as a guided example.)

When students are clear on the task, allow them 5 – 10 minutes to work.

Invite 3 – 5 students to share Learning Pit maps. Discuss.

Part II: How the Brain Builds Knowledge

Next, we are going to spend time learning about the science of learning.

View Video: "Your Brain is Like a Muscle"

https://ideas.classdojo.com/i/growth-mindset-1 (2:35)

Source: ClassDojo

Discussion Prompts*:

1. Do you agree that anyone can learn to become smarter? Why or why not?
2. Have you ever felt like Mojo? What would you say to a friend who was feeling like Mojo?
3. When Mojo is having trouble with the math problems, where would he be on the Learning Pit map?

*Adapted with permission from ClassDojo.

Closure

The Learning Pit map helps us remember that learning can be hard work. The video about Mojo helps us remember that even though learning is challenging, we can grow our brain and make it stronger by trying and practicing new things.

To wrap things up today, I want you to take a look at the essential questions guiding our learning journey.

Distribute exit slip (see Appendix A).

Lesson 3 Exit Slip

➢ **Think** about what we learned about learning today.

➢ **Review** the list of essential questions guiding our learning journey.

➢ **Reflect**: Which essential questions did our learning today connect to? Circle each question you believe today's learning responded to.

➢ **Respond**: Explain why you circled the questions you selected.

Essential Questions:

1. What is learning?
2. How do I know when I'm learning?
3. What makes a strong learner?
4. How do I plan and monitor a learning journey?

	Think: What did we learn from this lesson today? *Review:* Read the list of essential questions guiding our learning about learning journey. *Reflect*: Which essential questions did the lesson today connect to? Circle each question you believe today's learning responded to. *Respond*: Explain why you circled the questions you selected. Collect student responses. If time permits, invite students to share the connections they made.
Assessment	Review students' application of the Learning Pit (task 1). Gauge the degree to which they can identify themselves in each of the phases of a learning journey. Make note of any areas that seem to be unclear. Weave unclear areas into future lessons.
Special Note	There are many versions of the Learning Pit diagram available online. You can create your own on James Nottingham's website: https://www.challenginglearning.com/learning-pit/free-graphics/.

Lesson 4a: Mapping the Learning Pit – Jabari Jumps	
Overview	This lesson extends students' understanding of the Learning Pit by challenging them to map a storybook character's learning experience onto the Learning Pit map. There are 3 options for this lesson: a) Jabari Jumps, b) The Thing Lou Couldn't Do, and c) Andres and His Rubik's Cube Madness.
Learning Intention	I understand what learning is and how to use my awareness of the learning process to grow my knowledge and abilities.
Success Criteria	❑ I can reflect on a time I learned something new and explain how I knew I was learning. ❑ I can describe the difference between learning and practicing. ❑ I can respond to the question "Where does learning come from?" based on my own experience and storybook characters' experiences. ❑ I can use the Learning Pit to map and describe my journey as a learner. ❑ *I can use the Learning Pit to map and describe a storybook character's journey as a learner.* ❑ I can identify qualities of a strong learner. ❑ I understand how to use a progression to grow learner qualities. ❑ I can list learning goals I have this _____ (enter time duration here, i.e. week, month, quarter, trimester, semester). ❑ I can use the learning goal template to develop a plan to help me reach the learning goal I have identified. ❑ I can identify a learning tool, explain its purpose, and describe how to use it. ❑ I can select and use learning tools as part of a learning journey. ❑ I can participate in a Learning Talk to provide helpful feedback to another learner. ❑ I can use feedback from a Learning Talk to advance my progress toward a learning goal. ❑ I can use the progress monitoring template to assess my progress toward a learning goal.
Essential Questions	1. What is learning? 2. How do I know when I'm learning? 3. What makes a strong learner? 4. How do I plan and monitor a learning journey?

Materials	❑ Copy of the book *Jabari Jumps* by Gaia Cornwall
	JABARI JUMPS Gaia Cornwall
	❑ Empty copy of The Learning Pit (poster-size) ❑ Word cloud template (2 per student) ❑ Photo of each student (optional)
Instructional Strategies	• Read Aloud • Whole Class Discussion • Story Mapping • Learning Wall (Audit Trail)
Instructional Plan	**Introduction** *Last week we learned about something called the Learning Pit. I asked you to think about a time you learned something new and to map your journey onto a blank copy of the Learning Pit map.* *Today we are going to read a story about a boy named Jabari. In the story, Jabari is trying to learn something new. As we read, I want you to think about how Jabari's learning connects with what we learned about the Learning Pit.* (Read story.) **Application** *Now, let's think about Jabari's story using the Learning Pit map.* *Where (on the learning pit map) is Jabari at the beginning of the story? How do you know?* *When is Jabari thinking, "I wonder…I want to. I bet I can. This will be fun!"?* *When is Jabari thinking: "Whoa, this is more challenging than I expected! I'm not sure."?* *When might Jabari be thinking: "I can't do this. I don't get it. I may not good at this."*

When is Jabari thinking: "I'm starting to make sense of this. I think I can do it."

When is Jabari thinking: "I did it!"

When is Jabari thinking: "What have I learned from this? What can I learn next?"

As important as it is for us to be able to tell where <u>we</u>, ourselves, are on the Learning Pit map, it's also important to be able to tell where our friends and classmates are. This helps us know what we can do to support one another's learning.

Sometimes when we are learning something new, people do things that make it even harder for us to learn.
For example, when I was learning how to <u>(enter example here)</u>, someone said, "It's easy. Just <u>(contextualized example here)</u>" and that made me feel bad that I couldn't do it easily.

Now let's think about helping Jabari as a learner:
- ❑ Would it have been helpful if Jabari's dad just pushed him off the board the first time? Why or Why not?

- ❑ Would it have been helpful if Jabari's dad jumped off the board and said, "See, this is easy!"?

Task

Imagine you were with Jabari the first time he looked up the ladder to the diving board:
1. What would you say to Jabari to support him?
2. What would you say to Jabari to support *his learning*?

Write your words of support on the idea cloud. Use one cloud to record words of support for Jabari. Use the other cloud to record words that would support **his learning**.

Closure

Share word cloud examples.

When we support one another we say things like, "You can do it!" When we support someone else's learning it is helpful to say things that honor the difficulty that comes with learning something new.

	Some examples might be, "This will be a challenge, but I know you can try!" or "Just do your best. If you don't get it the first time, you can try again." Or "Let's think about a different strategy!"
	As we make our way through the year, let's use these words of support for one another. Let's help each other learn!
Assessment	Review word clouds. Create a wall display with the word cloud words of support. Include photos of each of your students and one of Jabari. Place the word clouds around the photos/images.
Special Note	*Due to copyright, images from *Jabari Jumps* are not included here. Recommended images are listed below. Corresponding placement on the Learning Pit map is indicated on the following page: Page 2: Jabari tells dad he's going off the diving board Page 4: Jabari says I'm not scared at all Page 6: Jabari squeezes dad's hand Page 7: Jabari looks up at the board Page 10: Jabari climbs the ladder Page 12: Jabari decides tomorrow will be better Page 14: Dad says it's ok to be scared Page 16: Jabari climbs Page 18: Jabari puts toes to the edge Page 21: Jabari jumps Page 24: Jabari hits the water Page 28 & 29: Double back flip is next.

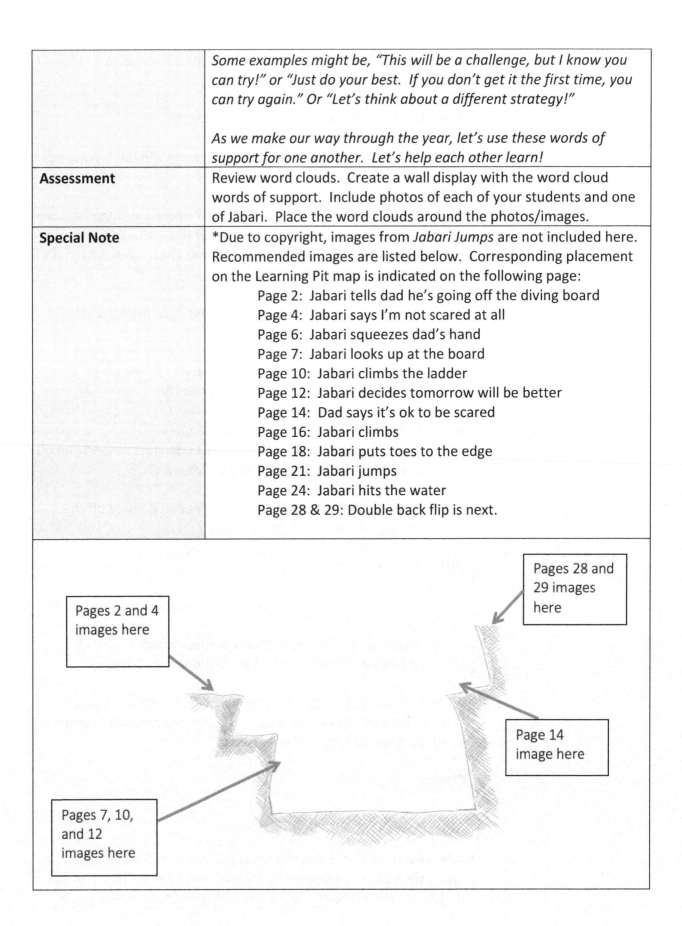

Pages 28 and 29 images here

Pages 2 and 4 images here

Page 14 image here

Pages 7, 10, and 12 images here

Lesson 4b: Mapping the Learning Pit – The Thing Lou Couldn't Do	
Overview	This lesson extends students' understanding of the Learning Pit by challenging them to map a storybook character's learning experience onto the Learning Pit map. There are 3 options for this lesson: a) Jabari Jumps, b) The Thing Lou Couldn't Do, and c) Andres and His Rubik's Cube Madness.
Learning Intention	I understand what learning is and how to use my awareness of the learning process to grow my knowledge and abilities.
Success Criteria	❑ I can reflect on a time I learned something new and explain how I knew I was learning.
	❑ I can describe the difference between learning and practicing.
	❑ I can respond to the question "Where does learning come from?" based on my own experience and storybook characters' experiences.
	❑ I can use the Learning Pit to map and describe my journey as a learner.
	❑ ***I can use the Learning Pit to map and describe a storybook character's journey as a learner.***
	❑ I can identify qualities of a strong learner.
	❑ I understand how to use a progression to grow learner qualities.
	❑ I can list learning goals I have this _____ (enter time duration here, i.e. week, month, quarter, trimester, semester).
	❑ I can use the learning goal template to develop a plan to help me reach the learning goal I have identified.
	❑ I can identify a learning tool, explain its purpose, and describe how to use it.
	❑ I can select and use learning tools as part of a learning journey.
	❑ I can participate in a Learning Talk to provide helpful feedback to another learner.
	❑ I can use feedback from a Learning Talk to advance my progress toward a learning goal.
	❑ I can use the progress monitoring template to assess my progress toward a learning goal.
Essential Questions	1. What is learning?
	2. How do I know when I'm learning?
	3. What makes a strong learner?
	4. How do I plan and monitor a learning journey?

Materials	☐ Copy of the book *The Thing Lou Couldn't Do* by Ashley Spires
	☐ Empty copy of the Learning Pit (poster-size)
	☐ Word cloud template (2 per student)
	☐ Photo of each student (optional)
Instructional Strategies	• Read Aloud
	• Whole Class Discussion
	• Story Mapping
	• Learning Wall (Audit Trail)
Instructional Plan	**Introduction**
	Last week we learned about something called the Learning Pit. I asked you to think about a time you learned something new and to map your journey onto a blank copy of the Learning Pit map.
	Today we are going to read a story about a girl named Lou. In the story, Lou is trying to learn something new. As we read, I want you to think about how Lou's learning connects with what we learned about the Learning Pit.
	(Read story.)
	Application
	Now, let's think about Lou's story using the Learning Pit map.
	Where (on the Learning Pit map) is Lou at the beginning of the story? How do you know?
	When is Lou thinking, "I wonder…I want to. I bet I can. This will be fun!"?
	When is Lou thinking: "Whoa, this is more challenging than I expected! I'm not sure."?
	When might Lou be thinking: "I can't do this. I don't get it. I may not good at this."

When is Lou thinking: "I'm starting to make sense of this. I think I can do it."

When is Lou thinking: "I did it!"

When is Lou thinking: "What have I learned from this? What can I learn next?"

As important as it is for us to be able to tell where <u>we</u>, ourselves, are on the Learning Pit map, it's also important to be able to tell where our friends and classmates are. This helps us know what we can do to support one another's learning.

Sometimes when we are learning something new, people do things that make it even harder for us to learn.

For example, when I was learning how to (<u>enter example here</u>), someone said, "It's easy. Just (<u>contextualized example here</u>)" and that made me feel bad that I couldn't do it easily.

Now let's think about Lou:
- ❑ Would it have been helpful if Lou's mom said, "That's ok, some people just aren't good at climbing trees?" Why or Why not?

- ❑ Would it have been helpful if Lou's friends hollered from the tree, "Lou can't even climb a tree!"

Task

Imagine you were with Lou the first time she looked up the tree and thought about climbing it:

1. What would you say to Lou to support her?
2. What would you say to Lou to support her learning?

Write your words of support on the idea cloud.

Closure

Share word cloud examples.

When we support one another we say things like, "You can do it!" When we support someone else's learning it is helpful to say things

	that honor the difficulty that comes with learning something new. Some examples might be, "This will be a challenge, but I know you can try!" or "Just do your best. If you don't get it the first time, you can try again." Or "Let's think about a different strategy!" *As we make our way through the year, let's use these words of support for one another. Let's help each other learn!*
Assessment	Review word clouds. Create a wall display with the word cloud words of support. Include photos of each of your students and one of Lou. Place the word clouds around the photos/images.

Special Note	*Due to copyright, images from *The Thing Lou Couldn't Do* are not included here. Recommended images and corresponding placement on the Learning Pit map are indicated below:
	        Page 2: Lou is brave with her friends.
	        Page 4: Lou looks up tree saying, "Umm…"
	        Page 5: Lou has never climbed a tree.
	        Page 7: Lou finds excuses not to climb.
	        Page 23: Lou tries to climb.
	        Page 26: Lou falls.
	        Page 27: Not yet.
	        Page 28: She'll be back. (to try again)

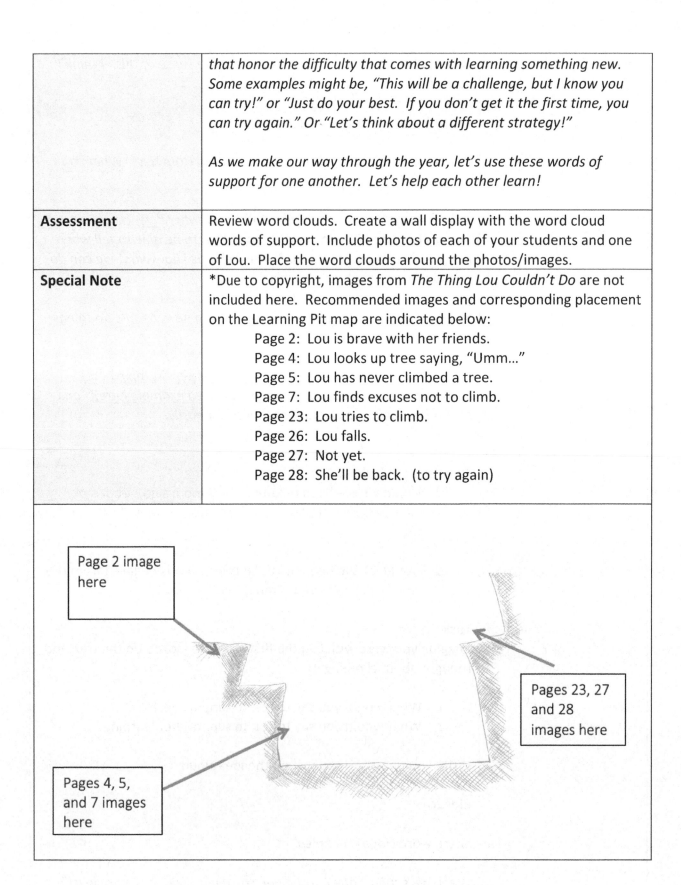

Page 2 image here

Pages 23, 27 and 28 images here

Pages 4, 5, and 7 images here

Lesson 4c: Mapping the Learning Pit – Andres and His Rubik's Cube Madness	
Overview	This lesson extends students' understanding of the Learning Pit by challenging them to map a storybook character's learning experience onto the Learning Pit map. There are 3 options for this lesson: a) Jabari Jumps, b) The Thing Lou Couldn't Do, and c) Andres and His Rubik's Cube Madness.
Learning Intention	I understand what learning is and how to use my awareness of the learning process to grow my knowledge and abilities.
Success Criteria	<ul><li>❏ I can reflect on a time I learned something new and explain how I knew I was learning.</li><li>❏ I can describe the difference between learning and practicing.</li><li>❏ I can respond to the question "Where does learning come from?" based on my own experience and storybook characters' experiences.</li><li>❏ I can use the Learning Pit to map and describe my journey as a learner.</li><li>❏ ***I can use the Learning Pit to map and describe a storybook character's journey as a learner.***</li><li>❏ I can identify qualities of a strong learner.</li><li>❏ I understand how to use a progression to grow learner qualities.</li><li>❏ I can list learning goals I have this _____ (enter time duration here, i.e. week, month, quarter, trimester, semester).</li><li>❏ I can use the learning goal template to develop a plan to help me reach the learning goal I have identified.</li><li>❏ I can identify a learning tool, explain its purpose, and describe how to use it.</li><li>❏ I can select and use learning tools as part of a learning journey.</li><li>❏ I can participate in a Learning Talk to provide helpful feedback to another learner.</li><li>❏ I can use feedback from a Learning Talk to advance my progress toward a learning goal.</li><li>❏ I can use the progress monitoring template to assess my progress toward a learning goal.</li></ul>
Essential Questions	1. What is learning? 2. How do I know when I'm learning? 3. What makes a strong learner? 4. How do I plan and monitor a learning journey?

Materials	❑ Copy of the book *Andres and His Rubik's Cube Madness* by Andrea Alvarez
	❑ Empty copy of the Learning Pit (poster-size)
	❑ Word cloud template (2 per student)
	❑ Photo of each student (optional)
Instructional Strategies	• Read Aloud
	• Whole Class Discussion
	• Story Mapping
	• Learning Wall (Audit Trail)
Instructional Plan	**Introduction**
	Last week we learned about something called the Learning Pit. I asked you to think about a time you learned something new and to map your journey onto a blank copy of the Learning Pit.
	Today we are going to read a story about a boy named Andres. In the story, Andres is trying to learn something new. As we read, I want you to think about how Andres's learning connects with what we learned about the Learning Pit.
	(Read story.)
	Application
	Now, let's think about Andres's story using the Learning Pit map.
	Where (on the learning pit map) is Andres at the beginning of the story? How do you know?
	When is Andres thinking, "I wonder...I want to. I bet I can. This will be fun!"?
	When is Andres thinking: "Whoa, this is more challenging than I expected! I'm not sure."?
	When might Andres be thinking: "I can't do this. I don't get it. I may not good at this."

When is Andres thinking: "I'm starting to make sense of this. I think I can do it."

When is Andres thinking: "I did it!"

When is Andres thinking: "What have I learned from this? What can I learn next?"

As important as it is for us to be able to tell where <u>we</u>, ourselves, are on the Learning Pit map, it's also important to be able to tell where our friends and classmates are. This helps us know what we can do to support one another's learning.

Sometimes when we are learning something new, people do things that make it even harder for us to learn.

For example, when I was learning how to (<u>enter example here</u>), someone said, "It's easy. Just (<u>contextualized example here</u>)" and that made me feel bac that I couldn't do it easily.

Now let's think about Andres:

- ❑ Would it have been helpful if Kino said, "Here, I'll just do it for you." when Andres asked how to solve a Rubik's cube? Why or Why not?

- ❑ Would it have been helpful if Andres' mom told him solving a Rubik's cube is impossible or just too hard?

Task
Imagine you were with Andres the first time he was trying to solve the Rubik's cube:
1. What would you say to Andres to support him?
2. What would you say to Andres to support *his learning?*

Write your words of support on the idea cloud.

Closure
Share word cloud examples.

When we support someone we say things like, "You can do it!" or "You've got this!" When we support someone else's learning it is helpful to say things that honor the difficulty that comes with learning something new. Some examples might be, "This will be a challenge,

	but I know you can try!" or "Just do your best. If you don't get it the first time, you can try again." Or "Let's think about a different strategy!" *As we make our way through the year, let's use these words of support for one another. Let's help each other learn!*
Assessment	Review word clouds. Create a wall display with the word cloud words of support. Include photos of each of your students and one of Andres. Place the word clouds around the photos/images.
Special Note	*Due to copyright, images from *Andres and His Rubik's Cube Madness* are not included here. Recommended images are listed below. Corresponding placement on the Learning Pit map is indicated on the following page: Page 4: Andres is curious about the Rubik's cube Page 6: Andres says, "This is impossible!" Page 7: Andres's mom says, "You can do anything you set your mind to, but you must work hard." Page 10: Andres practices all the time. Page 11: Andres solves the cube! Now he wants to solve it faster. Page 13: Andres studies algorithms to improve his time. Page 20: Andres is frustrated because the cube breaks. Page 22: Andres and Kino practice together. Page 23: Andres is not sure he is fast enough for the competition. Page 30: Andres solved the cube in 15 seconds. Page 34: Now he wonders if he could compete in the national cubing championship.

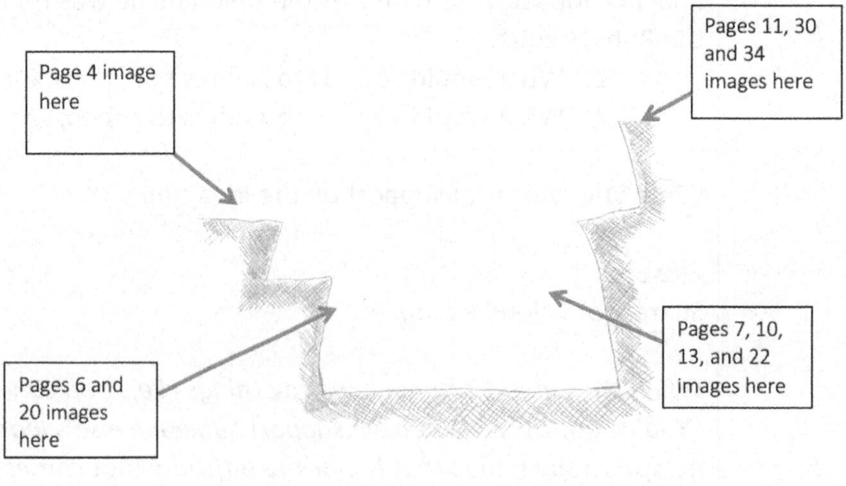

Page 4 image here

Pages 11, 30 and 34 images here

Pages 6 and 20 images here

Pages 7, 10, 13, and 22 images here

Chapter Three: Learner Qualities

It doesn't take long to realize that fostering an understanding of the learning process is not a "one and done" method for helping people learn about learning. It is one thing to understand the pattern of learning. It is another thing to understand what attributes make someone effective at navigating the terrain of a learning journey. Left unchecked, many people – young and old alike – are prone to thinking that persons who can play a guitar, read a book, or run a marathon are inherently better at these tasks than others. Of course, this is not true.

As Malcom Gladwell (2008) explored in his book, *Outliers,* the people who are really good at a task – be it playing hockey, programming computers, or singing opera – acquired their strength in each of these domains by learning and practicing and learning again. Gladwell's studies found that the *really great* invested at least 10,000 hours in a particular domain (Gladwell, 2008). But even this oversimplifies the equation a bit. Another factor that contributes to a person's strength at a particular task is the set of learning dispositions s/he brings to each learning opportunity, the qualities of being a powerful learner. ***What are these qualities, and how do we help learners grow them?***

There are two models I have found especially useful in working to respond to the questions above. Each is based on the idea of "dispositions of learning" (Costa & Kallick, 2014). At the Stonefields School in Auckland, New Zealand (an exemplar of theory-to-practice schooling), the learning culture is constructed around a collection of seven learner qualities: ***Reflect, Question, Connect, Think, Be Self-Aware, Wonder*** and ***Be Determined.*** The school's philosophy centers upon helping students thrive in the face of uncertain or complex situations; helping students learn how to learn. School leaders introduce the learner qualities gradually across the course of a school year. Students then monitor their progress around each of the seven learner qualities using progressions (more on this later) during their tenure at the school.

In another model, cognitive scientist, Guy Claxton, refers to learner qualities as "the elements of learning power" (Claxton, 2018, p. 107). In Claxton's model, the essential attributes are ***Curiosity, Attention, Determination, Imagination, Thinking, Socializing, Reflection,*** and ***Organization*** (Claxton, 2018). Claxton believes the best thing we can do for students is to teach learners to teach themselves. His "Learning Power Approach" aims to build in all students the confidence and capacities of being a good learner so they can be successful, individually and collaboratively, in school and beyond (Claxton, 2018).

No matter which framework you select, it is important for learners to understand that there are specific qualities that lead to more efficient and effective learning. More important yet, it is essential that students understand how to grow these capacities within themselves. There are five distinct but interdependent ways we can accomplish this: 1. Explicit instruction, 2. Progressions, 3. Embedded Application, 4. Self-Directed Learning, and 5. Metacognitive Reflection.

Explicit Instruction

While children are by nature learners, the dispositions of learning will not necessarily cultivate themselves. Educators are advised to design learning opportunities – interventions – that explicitly focus on each of the learner qualities (Costa & Kallick, 2014; Hattie, 2009). Such opportunities challenge students to examine the nature, value, and purpose of a learner quality as applied to a learning task. For example, if students are challenged to build the tallest standing structure they can with a limited set of resources, they can later reflect on the role determination played on their progress. Then, in the future, they can extend that common experience and resultant reflection to predict how determination will impact their ability to complete a science investigation, run a mile, or read a challenging book.

Progressions

Progressions are tools developed to assist students in monitoring their own growth toward a learning goal. Applied to learner qualities, progressions help students gain a clearer understanding of how a learner quality evolves across a continuum of time and complexity. Consider a progression for the learner quality "Question" (see page 45). At the beginning of a school year a student may only ask a question when a teacher prompts her to. As the year progresses, she may advance to adding questions to a "Wonder Wall" without prompting. Using the Question Progression as a learning tool, the student can set goals of asking questions throughout a learning journey, prioritizing questions according to interest or testability, and working with others to ask and respond to questions. The Question Progression serves as a visible reminder of how to grow her capacity around this specific learner quality.

As example, school leaders at the Stonefields School in New Zealand developed a set of progressions to help students monitor their progress around each of the seven learner qualities the school curriculum is grounded on. Each progression spans roughly eight years of development. At Stonefields, the final destination is "part of me" status which intends to convey that an attribute is so engrained in a learner it is actually a part of their being. Sample progressions for "Being Determined" and "Making Connections" can be found within Lessons 5 and 6. These are adapted from the model developed by educators at Stonefields School.

Embedded Application

In addition to explicit instruction around a specific learner quality, students should be given frequent and sustained opportunities to utilize the quality within complex learning tasks. These instances challenge students to draw upon learner qualities in times of authentic need. Students may employ a learner quality on their own, or they may benefit from prompting: *"How can you use what you know about making connections to help you respond to this challenge?"* Either way, use of the learner quality in a novel situation helps build a student's "inclinations, sensitivities, and abilities" around the quality of focus (Perkins, Jay & Tishman, 1993, p. 2).

Self-Directed Learning

One of the most important and often overlooked components of learner quality development is providing students time, space, and opportunity to define and work toward their own learning goals. The soccer player who wants to improve her shot, the fourth grader who wants to learn how to repair his bike, the sixth grader who wants to learn how to make a stained-glass window – each is motivated by a natural desire to learn and/or improve. Allowing students to engage in tasks that are interesting and useful to them often draws upon and develops learner qualities more robustly than prescribed tasks may accomplish on their own. Whether Passion Projects, Breakthrough, Genius Hour, or simply working on a project in the backyard, self-directed learning cultivates the development of learner qualities under conditions of intrinsic motivation.

Metacognitive Reflection

Finally, it is important to challenge learners to explicitly reflect on when, where, why, and how a specific learner quality served a particular purpose on a learning journey. This action fosters metacognitive awareness in students that can be applied to future learning endeavors, feeding forward to increase a student's capacity around each learner quality of focus.

Summary

We do not know what the future holds or which personal or academic skills will be of most value to our youth down the road. This makes it less important for students to master content ("knowing") and more important for them to master learning. Rest assured, learner qualities do not get in the way of academic or athletic standards. Instead, they are the foundation on which all learning is built.

The lessons that follow assist students in reflecting on the following questions:

> *What are the qualities that make a strong learner?*

> *How do I grow these qualities in myself?*

> *How do I support the growth of these qualities in others?*

Note:
Before facilitating Lesson 5, determine if you prefer for students to identify learner qualities collaboratively, if you wish to introduce specific qualities to them, or if you plan to utilize a combination of both approaches.

The lessons that follow introduce learner qualities and guide students to develop an understanding of the "Be Determined" and "Make Connections" qualities. The format serves as a model for other qualities you opt to focus on.

Question

"I ask questions to grow myself as a learner."

Not Yet	Beginning		Developing			Applying		Proficient
I do not ask questions.	**I ask a question if someone tells me to.**	**I can use different words to start my questions.**	**I use connections to build a question.**	**I ask questions throughout a learning journey.**	**I can distinguish between open and closed questions.**	**I can prioritize questions.**	**I can ask a question and I know what to do with the question to move toward an answer.**	**I can work with others to ask and respond to questions.**
	I add ideas to the wonder wall.	I can ask "why?" questions.	I can ask questions that connect to the **world.**	I ask questions **before** a learning opportunity.	I can identify open questions.	I can identify the most important questions from a list.	I use questions to plan a project.	I use questions to identify a problem.
	I add questions to my wonder journal.	I can ask "when?" questions.	I can ask questions that connect to a **text.**	I ask questions **during** a learning opportunity.	I can identify closed questions.	I can identify the most interesting questions from a list.	I use questions to organize my work.	I use questions to develop a plan to solve a problem.
	I ask questions during class discussions.	I can ask "how?" questions.	I can ask questions that connect to my **peers.**	I ask questions **after** a learning opportunity.	I can write open questions.	I can identify the questions that will be most helpful to my project (from a list).	I use questions to improve my work.	I use questions to identify my role on a team project.
		I can ask "where?" questions.	I can ask questions that connect to **different classes.**		I can write closed questions.	I can identify questions that are testable from a list.		I use questions to reflect on the quality of my work on a team project.
		I can ask "what?" questions.				I can explain my reason for choosing a question.		I use questions to improve my team's work.
		I can ask "who?" questions.						

Adapted from Stonefields School, www.stonefields.school.nz ; *Image Source:* stock.adobe.com/sonaldo.

Chapter Four: "Learner Quality" Lessons

Lesson 5: Introduction to Learner Qualities	
Overview	This lesson introduces students to the idea of learner qualities: attributes that lead to strong learning.
Learning Intention	I understand what learning is and how to use my awareness of the learning process to grow my knowledge and abilities.
Success Criteria	❑ I can reflect on a time I learned something new and explain how I knew I was learning. ❑ I can describe the difference between learning and practicing. ❑ I can respond to the question "Where does learning come from?" based on my own experience and storybook characters' experiences. ❑ I can use the Learning Pit to map and describe my journey as a learner. ❑ I can use the Learning Pit to map and describe a storybook character's journey as a learner. ❑ *I can identify qualities of a strong learner.* ❑ *I can use a progression to grow the "Be Determined" quality.* ❑ I can list learning goals I have this _____ (enter time duration here, i.e. week, month, quarter, trimester, semester). ❑ I can use the learning goal template to develop a plan to help me reach the learning goal I have identified. ❑ I can identify a learning tool, explain its purpose, and describe how to use it. ❑ I can select and use learning tools as part of a learning journey. ❑ I can participate in a Learning Talk to provide helpful feedback to another learner. ❑ I can use feedback from a Learning Talk to advance my progress toward a learning goal. ❑ I can use the progress monitoring template to assess my progress toward a learning goal.
Essential Questions	1. What is learning? 2. How do I know when I'm learning? 3. What makes a strong learner? 4. How do I plan and monitor a learning journey?

Materials	❑ Learning Pit (poster or projection) ❑ Cover images (Appendix A page 108); 1 per student OR projection ❑ Smart Board for viewing videos ❑ "Be Determined" poster ❑ "Be Determined" progression (1 per student) ❑ "Be Determined" exit slip (1 per student)
Instructional Strategies	• Think-Pair-Share • Disposition Intervention • Direct Instruction • Self-Assessment • Learning Wall (Audit Trail)
Instructional Plan	**Part I: Introduction to Learner Qualities** *Throughout the past few weeks, we been on a journey to learn about learning.* (Retrace steps on Learning Wall if you are using one. See page 150 for details.) *We spent time thinking about things we've learned and how we knew we were learning.* *We reflected on and responded to the question "Where does learning come from?"* *And we were introduced to the pattern of learning through a model James Nottingham developed called the "Learning Pit."* *Today we are going to continue the journey by thinking about what makes a strong learner. I want to start by asking you to study a set of images.* Project page 110 on screen.

Application

Do you see evidence of learning in these pictures, or not? Explain your thinking.

Allow time for students to record their ideas.

Image 1:
Let's look at this one (point to image of girl crossing the monkey bars).

Has anyone here learned to cross the monkey bars?
What did you have to do to master this challenge?
What did you have to be to master this challenge?.

What are some things you might be thinking when you are learning to cross the monkey bars?

Record responses on chart paper. Possible responses include:
- How do I do this?
- If I keep trying, I will get better.
- I can't do this.
- This is hard!
- My hands hurt!
- If I take a break, I can try again.

Which of these ways of thinking would be particularly helpful to you as a learner?

Which of these ways of thinking might not be so useful to you as a learner?

Image 2:
Let's look at this one (point to the image of boy jumping rope).

Has anyone here learned to jump rope?
What did you have to do to master this challenge?
What did you have to be to master this challenge?

Note: Select images that are the best fit for your group of students.

As I stated earlier, this week we are going to shift our focus to the question: **What makes a strong learner?**

Learning requires us to develop qualities that help us make our way through the entire learning journey.

Trace through the Learning Pit poster to convey this idea.

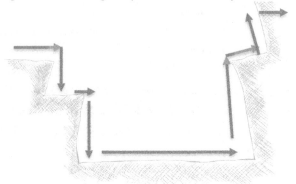

People who study learning and the human brain call these qualities Learner Qualities or Learner Dispositions. They are characteristics – ways of being and ways of thinking – that help learners develop new knowledge and abilities.

Part II: Be Determined

Today we are going to spend some time exploring the part of a learning journey when you feel stuck. Let's look at this place down here (point to the "I am confused," "I'm stuck," and "I don't know what to do" area of the map.

Think about a time you've felt this way when learning something new.

Think-Pair-Share

What does it take to move past this stuck, confused, "I don't know what to do" place?

> What **quality** makes a strong learner here?

One quality that is important to strong learners is determination: Believing that you can move past the stuck place. Knowing that, even if you don't know how to do something now, you can get better with additional time and practice.

Today we are going to watch two videos that will add to our understanding of what it means to be determined. The first video is called "The Magic of Mistakes." As you watch, think about how mistakes can help you learn.

Video 1: "The Magic of Mistakes" (2:58).
https://ideas.classdojo.com/i/growth-mindset-2

Discussion:
1. How can we learn from our mistakes? Share a specific example from your life.

The second video is called "The Incredible Power of Yet".

Video 2: "The Incredible Power of Yet" (2:32)
https://ideas.classdojo.com/i/growth-mindset-3

Video Source: ClassDojo

Discussion:

2. Why is the word "yet" so important when it comes to learning?

*Discussion questions adapted with permission from Class DoJo. For additional questions provided by ClassDojo use the link below:
https://ideas.classdojo.com/f/growth-mindset-3/1

Part III: Growing the "Be Determined" Quality

<u>Teaching Note</u>: In this portion of the lesson, the goal is to help students understand how they could grow the learner quality "Be Determined". There are at least two ways to approach this:
1. Provide them with a progression you've created similar to the one below, or
2. Challenge them to co-create a progression for your classroom community.

The plans that follow address option 1 above.

Being Determined is a quality that helps learners make their way through the stuck places of learning challenges. As a student, it's important to think about how you can grow this quality in yourself. One tool that is helpful is called a progression. A progression shows how a learner quality progresses from a beginner level to more advanced levels.

Let's look at a sample progression for "Be Determined":

Be Determined

"I do not give up when I am faced with a challenge."

Beginning	Developing	Area of Strength
If something is challenging, I usually give up.	If something is challenging, I will try a couple times but then I give up.	I know if I keep trying I will get better at the task.
I will say if something is too hard. I can recognize the challenge.	If someone helps me, I will stick with a task.	If one strategy does not work, I know I can try another.
	If someone helps me, I will try to find a new strategy to work on the challenge.	I keep trying until I find my way through a challenge.

Adapted from: Stonefields School https://www.stonefields.school.nz/

Think about yourself as a learner. Look at the progression for "Be Determined".
- ➤ What do you do when you are stuck in a learning task or challenge?
- ➤ Do you have a tendency to say, "I am going to stick with this" or do you have a tendency to say, "This is just too hard" or "I don't get it"?
- ➤ Are there types of tasks you are more likely to be determined about than others? If yes, what kinds of learning are you more likely to be determined about? What are you more likely to give up on?

How would you rate yourself right now on this progression?
Put an "X" in each box that describes you right now.

Closure

Now that you know more about the "Be Determined" learner quality, let's close our "learning about learning" time today with a reflection. Take a few minutes to read, reflect and respond to one of the following prompts.

1. *Describe a time you enacted the "Be Determined" learner quality this week. How did being determined help you and your learning?*

    OR

2. *Describe a time this week that would have benefited from the "Be Determined" learner quality. How would the experience have changed if you used the "Be Determined" quality?*

K – 2:

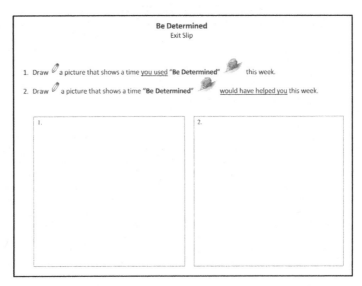

3 – 8:

Be Determined
Exit Slip

1. Describe a time you enacted the "Be Determined" learner quality this week. How did being determined help you and your learning?

   OR

2. Describe a time that would have benefited from the "Be Determined" learner quality this week. How would the experience have changed if you used the "Be Determined" quality?

	Optional Extension
	Invite students to complete the "Tallest Standing Structure" task using a limited set of resources. Following the task, spend time reflecting on how "Being Determined" effected each team's progress.
Assessment	Collect students' self-assessments of their current status on the "Be Determined" learner quality rubric. Collect exit slip reflections. Revisit the rubrics throughout the year as students work on learning projects.
Special Note	For additional resources on learner qualities, see the bibliography at the end of this guide.

Lesson 6: Learner Qualities (continued)	
Overview	This lesson continues exploration of learner qualities.
Learning Intention	I understand what learning is and how to use my awareness of the learning process to grow my knowledge and abilities.
Success Criteria	❑ I can reflect on a time I learned something new and explain how I knew I was learning. ❑ I can describe the difference between learning and practicing. ❑ I can respond to the question "Where does learning come from?" based on my own experience and storybook characters' experiences. ❑ I can use the Learning Pit to map and describe my journey as a learner. ❑ I can use the Learning Pit to map and describe a storybook character's journey as a learner. ❑ *I can identify qualities of a strong learner.* ❑ *I can use a progression to grow the "Connect" quality.* ❑ I can list learning goals I have this _____ (enter time duration here, i.e. week, month, quarter, trimester, semester). ❑ I can use the learning goal template to develop a plan to help me reach the learning goal I have identified. ❑ I can identify a learning tool, explain its purpose, and describe how to use it. ❑ I can select and use learning tools as part of a learning journey. ❑ I can participate in a Learning Talk to provide helpful feedback to another learner. ❑ I can use feedback from a Learning Talk to advance my progress toward a learning goal. ❑ I can use the progress monitoring template to assess my progress toward a learning goal.
Essential Questions	1. What is learning? 2. How do I know when I'm learning? 3. What makes a strong learner? 4. How do I plan and monitor a learning journey?
Materials	❑ Smart Board for viewing videos ❑ Making Connections: What is a neuron? (1 per student) ❑ Additional source of information about neurons* (see list at end of lesson plan for possibilities) ❑ "Connect" poster ❑ "Connect" progression (1 copy per student)

Instructional Strategies	• Think-Pair-Share • Direct Instruction • Learner Quality Intervention • Self-Assessment • Learning Wall (Audit Trail)
Instructional Plan	**Part I: Introduction to Learner Quality #2 – Connect** *Another quality that is important to strong learners is **making connections**.* *When we think about how <u>what we already know</u> connects to <u>new learning experience</u>s, we deepen and strengthen understanding.* *Today we are going to watch a video that helps us understand what happens in our brains when we work to make connections as we learn. As you watch, think about the question: What is a neuron?* **Application** <u>View Video</u>: **"The Mysterious World of Neurons"** (2:49) Link https://ideas.classdojo.com/i/growth-mindset-4 Source: Class Dojo (link included with permission) <u>Discussion</u>: After the video, ask students to respond to the questions below: 1. What is a neuron? (Have students record their response to this question on puzzle piece 1 of the "What is a neuron?" recording page.) Then, discuss the following together: 2. How do we make connections between our neurons? 3. Describe a time you made a new connection in your brain. How do you know a connection was made?

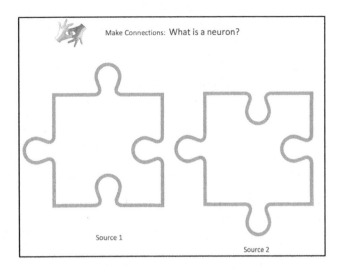

Questions adapted from static.classdojo.com/docs/Big Ideas/BigIdeas_episode4_discussion guide.pdf (links included with permission)

Next, have students learn about neurons from another source. Possibilities include:

- *The Neuron* by Dr. Thomai Dion
- *How Learning Works* from KidsDiscover
- Science textbook

*Next, we are going to learn about neurons from another source of information. We will read the book "The Neuron." As we read, think about how what you are learning from this source **connects to** what you learned from Mojo.*

Challenge students to make a connection between the two sources of information about neurons.

1. What is a neuron?
   (Have students record their response to this question on puzzle piece 2 of the "What is a neuron?" recording page.)

Then,

2. How does a neuron carry messages for the brain?
3. How do we make connections between our neurons?
4. How does making connections help us as learners?

How does our learning grow when we make connections?

Part II: Growing the "Connect" Quality

A sample progression for Making Connections is provided on the following page. Use it as a stand-alone, or as a starting point from which your class can develop a more fully fleshed out, context-based progression.

Next, think about yourself as a learner. Look at the progression for the Learner Quality "Connect".

Connect

"I link prior knowledge and new thinking together to create new understandings."

Beginning	Developing	Area of Strength
I do not usually think about how old learning connects with new learning.	I can make simple connections between one idea and another idea.	I work hard to make connections between my knowledge and new learning.
Sometimes I make a simple connection between old learning and new learning.	If someone helps me, I will try to think about how my knowledge connects to new learning.	I work to make connections between ideas even if they do not seem related.
		I make connections between what I am learning in one class and what I am learning in another class.
		I make connections to deepen my understanding.

Adapted from: Stonefields School https://www.stonefields.school.nz/

1. *When you are learning something new, do you link knowledge and thinking together to create new understandings?*
2. *Do you think about what you are learning in math connects with what you are learning in science?*

How would you rate yourself right now on this progression? Why?

Closure

Throughout the weeks ahead we will work to grow the "Connect" learner quality. Be on the lookout for ways you can connect prior knowledge to new thinking.

Optional Extension:

One way to foster metacognition around the "Connect" learner quality is to invite students to record connections they make on blank puzzle pieces. Later, gather as a class to assemble the

	Connections Puzzle and display it as a reminder of the value of this learner quality.
Assessment	Collect students' self-assessments of their current status on the "Connect" learner quality rubric.
Special Note	*Additional sources of information on neurons include: • "The Neuron" by Dr. Thomai Dion • "The Brain" by Simon Seymour • "How Learning Works" from KidsDiscover

Chapter Five: Planning and Monitoring a Learning Journey

The final step in helping students learn how to learn is apprenticing them to the process of planning and monitoring a learning journey. Most often, teachers are assigned the responsibility of instructional planning and facilitation of learning. If we are not careful, though, teachers can overstep these bounds and take the reins from students, leaving them less cognizant of where a learning journey is headed, why they are on that particular journey, and how they are doing with regard to progress toward the final destination. This can lead to a brand of passivity within students that lessens the learning power of tasks and activities across all disciplines. When students' perceived rationale for completing a task is "to get it done" or "because Mr./Ms. ____ said I have to," we can be reasonably confident the learning goals of the task have been diminished.

To promote a model of learning within which students are actively engaged with the purpose, direction, and outcomes of a learning journey, we are wise to foster the development of "assessment capable learners" (Absolum et al., 2009; Frey, Fisher & Hattie, 2018). This descriptor does not intend to convey that students must perform well on assessments, but rather that learners are capable of assessing their own progress toward learning goals, identifying what they have done well and/or where they need more work or extra help, and using feedback to refine or adjust course (Absolum et al., 2009; Absolum, 2010; Frey, Fisher & Hattie, 2018).

Fostering the development of assessment capable learners means *helping students learn how to learn*. But, how do we do this? Research suggests explicit attention to the following elements of instruction (Absolum et al., 2009; Absolum, 2010; Frey, Fisher, & Hattie, 2018; Wiliam, 2016):

- Learning Intentions
- Success Criteria
- Relevance Statements
- Assessment
- Learning Tools
- Progress Monitoring
- Feedback

The paragraphs that follow offer a brief explanation of each element. Then, Lessons 7 through 10 operationalize the ideas in a student-friendly manner. The lessons are intended to be utilized over and over again as students develop their capacity for planning and monitoring learning journeys.

Learning Intentions, Success Criteria & Relevance Statements

Learning objectives or learning targets have long been a part of instructional planning. In early iterations, it was believed important for teachers to have clarity around a lesson's objective. In more recent times, teachers are expected to post this information so students can clearly see it. Sometimes students are asked to read the learning intentions aloud prior to beginning a lesson or task. What is not always as clear to learners, however, is why the objectives exist, how they connect to prior learning experiences, and how they will connect to learning that will follow. In *Clarity in the Classroom: Using formative assessment for building learning-focused relationships* Michael Absolum (2010) suggests that educators should always be clear about three aspects of learning:

1. **<u>Learning Intentions</u>**
2. **<u>Success Criteria</u>**
3. **<u>Relevance</u>**

Each of these elements can be considered critical signposts that point learners toward meta-cognitive awareness and improved coherence within learning endeavors. For Absolum, "Learning intentions describe what we want students to learn or what it is that students want to or need to learn" (Absolum, 2010, p. 82). Success criteria help students understand how we — and they — will know if they are making progress toward the learning intention. Finally, relevance statements provide clarity about *why* something is to be learned and *how* it matters in the context of daily life.

For example, the learning intention, success criteria and relevance statements for the lessons contained in this book are as follows:

Learning Intention: I understand what learning is and how to use my understanding of the learning process to grow my knowledge and abilities.

Success Criteria:

- ❑ I can reflect on a time I learned something new and explain how I knew I was learning.
- ❑ I can describe the difference between learning and practicing.
- ❑ I can respond to the question "Where does learning come from?" based on my own experience and storybook characters' experiences.
- ❑ I can use the Learning Pit to map and describe my journey as a learner.
- ❑ I can use the Learning Pit to map and describe a storybook character's journey as a learner.
- ❑ I can identify qualities of a strong learner.
- ❑ I can use a progression to grow learner qualities.
- ❑ I can list learning goals I have this _____ (enter time duration here, i.e. week, month, quarter, trimester, semester).
- ❑ I can use the learning goal template to develop a plan to help me reach the learning goal I have identified.
- ❑ I can identify a learning tool, explain its purpose, and describe how to use it.
- ❑ I can select and use learning tools as part of a learning journey.
- ❑ I can participate in a Learning Talk to provide helpful feedback to another learner.
- ❑ I can use feedback from a Learning Talk to advance my progress toward a learning goal.

❏ I can use the progress monitoring template to assess my progress toward a learning goal.

Relevance: As I grow, I will need to build new knowledge and learn how to do new things. Understanding how to learn will help me grow my abilities as a student, athlete, artist, friend, and more.

When we are clear about a learning opportunity's intentions, success criteria and relevance, students are better able to engage with the opportunity. In addition, they are more likely to think in a meta-cognitive manner about how the learning connects with the framework of their lived lives. When students can connect learning in school to life outside of school, the learning is more likely to be picked up, utilized, and last.

Assessment

Once a learning goal – or learning intention – has been identified, the next step is typically pre-assessment; figuring out what students know before beginning the next lesson or unit of study. Very often responsibility for pre-assessment has fallen to teachers. At a minimum, teachers are expected to document students' understanding at the beginning of a unit and at the end of the unit, then report resultant gains in student learning. Unfortunately, assigning responsibility for assessment solely to teachers can be a misstep in terms of helping students learn how to learn. When we position students in a passive role within the assessment process, we can diminish learning potential. Students are denied the opportunity to actively reflect on what knowledge they bring to a new learning experience, how that compares with what they want or need to know, and what steps they can take to close the gap between current capacity and the desired learning goal. Instead of beginning a learning journey with a clear roadmap from start to finish, they may wander somewhat aimlessly with no clear sense of where they're going or why.

Assessment capable learners understand the importance of pausing to assess where they are, where they're heading, and what ground must be covered to bridge the gap. Teachers who foster the development of assessment capable learners purposely afford students the time and scaffolding necessary to grow this awareness.

Learning Tools

If learning is the construction of knowledge and abilities, it follows that having a collection of tools readily accessible is important for learners. The process of matching a learning outcome with an instructional strategy (tool) is typically a responsibility assigned to the teacher. Here again, if an understanding of which learning tool is best for a given task resides solely with the teacher, learning power for students is reduced. Assessment capable learners need to be able to decide which tools to try as they navigate their way through a learning journey. This requires students to actively select, utilize, and assess the effectiveness of a variety of learning tools. Helping students develop the capacity to select from a repertoire of tools is accomplished through a delicate balance of explicit instruction around the purpose and use of a learning tool *and* freedom to experiment with the tools as applied to unique stages of a learning journey.

A final point worth mention: Robust tool sets are borne of a net cast wide. Learning tools – ways of knowing – come from a variety of sources: peers, parents, community experts, authors, and more. Allowing students the opportunity to develop decision-making skills about the use of learning tools enables them to be and become independent learners.

Feedback

In simplest terms, feedback is "information about how we are doing in our efforts to reach a goal" (Wiggins, 2012, p. 10). When applied to learning, feedback is one of the most effective tools we have to support a learner in a differentiated manner. Though not all feedback is equally effective.

Research indicates feedback is most useful when it is timely, specific, actionable, and understandable (Frey, Fisher, & Hattie, 2018). The most valuable feedback clearly addresses what the learning goal is *("Where am I going?")*, what progress has been made toward the goal *("How am I going?"),* and what next steps might be taken to close the gap between current capacities and the desired outcome *(Where to next?")* (Hattie & Timperley, 2007). Feedback is optimized when it is provided *during* – not just at the end of – a learning journey. This enables students to utilize the feedback in an "on demand" manner, shaping learning in the moment.

The ultimate goal of feedback, however, is to improve students' ability to perform on tasks they have not yet encountered. For example, if I review a second grade student's work and note that he needs to remember to capitalize the first word of every sentence and include a punctuation mark at the end it is not sufficient for him to quickly edit the work that revealed this area for growth. Instead, I need to challenge him to think about a way he can remember to carry this feedback forward into future tasks. In this way, feedback becomes a learning tool students pack in their learning journey knapsack. Assessment capable learners recognize the value of feedback in helping them reach their goals

Including students in the process of providing feedback – whether to themselves or peers – requires explicit instruction around the features of constructive feedback. Instead of simply prompting students to give one another advice about their work, a gradual release of responsibility scaffolded by carefully constructed prompts yields more valuable guidance and gains in learning both about and from feedback. This can be accomplished with students in the primary grades ("*One compliment I have is…*" "*One suggestion I have is…*") as well as the middle grades and beyond *("A strength of your work is…"*, "*An area for growth is…"*) Feedback can and should come from a variety of sources: teacher, peers, self, parent(s), and community experts.

Finally, making time for collaborative feedback sessions increases the odds that students practice the language of learning. The protocols included within Lesson 8 help students talk the discourse of learning into being. This heightens awareness around the role mistakes, tools, and feedback play in the learning process.

Progress Monitoring

An essential part of the goal-setting process is monitoring one's progress toward an identified goal. Learning is rarely a linear endeavor and, if we are not careful, students can lose sight of a learning goal while in the midst of a learning journey. To guard against this tendency, it is helpful to confer with students on a routine basis to discuss the progress they've made toward a specific learning goal. An essential part of the conversation should challenge students to distinguish between the strategies they've used that have worked and those that have proven ineffective. In addition, students should identify the next steps they will take to continue progress toward the learning goal. Lesson 10 introduces students a template to assist them in monitoring progress toward a learning goal. Page _____ in Appendix A consists of a protocol to guide conferring sessions.

In Summary

Fostering the development of assessment capable learners means helping students learn how to learn. The lessons that follow are designed to help students develop fluency with the process of designing and monitoring a learning journey. It is worth noting that learning journeys can be passion projects or aligned to academic standards. The templates provided work well for either style.

Chapter Six: "Planning & Monitoring a Learning Journey" Lessons

Lesson 7: Setting Learner Goals	
Overview	This lesson challenges students to create and manage a learning goal for themselves.
Learning Intention	I understand what learning is and how to use my awareness of the learning process to grow my knowledge and abilities.
Success Criteria	❑ I can reflect on a time I learned something new and explain how I knew I was learning. ❑ I can describe the difference between learning and practicing. ❑ I can respond to the question "Where does learning come from?" based on my own experience and storybook characters' experiences. ❑ I can use the Learning Pit to map and describe my journey as a learner. ❑ I can use the Learning Pit to map and describe a storybook character's journey as a learner. ❑ I can identify qualities of a strong learner. ❑ I can use a progression to grow learner qualities. ❑ *I can list learning goals I have this _____ (enter time duration here, i.e. week, month, quarter, trimester, semester).* ❑ *I can use the learning goal template to develop a plan to help me reach the learning goal I have identified.* ❑ I can identify a learning tool, explain its purpose, and describe how to use it. ❑ I can select and use learning tools as part of a learning journey. ❑ I can participate in a Learning Talk to provide helpful feedback to another learner. ❑ I can use feedback from a Learning Talk to advance my progress toward a learning goal. ❑ I can use the progress monitoring template to assess my progress toward a learning goal.
Essential Questions	1. What is learning? 2. How do I know when I'm learning? 3. What makes a strong learner? 4. How do I plan and monitor a learning journey?
Materials	• Sample standards/benchmarks. • Video projection • Goal Setting Template (1 copy per student) • Anchor chart copy of Goal Setting Template

Instructional Strategies	• Message abundancy • Direct Instruction • Gradual Release of Responsibility • Learning Wall (Audit Trail)
Instructional Plan	**Part I: Introduction to Goals** *One thing strong learners do is think about ways they can grow. Today we are going to spend some time talking about learning goals, why they are important in life, and how the goals we set help us grow in and beyond school. We will also work to identify a learning goal you have for yourself and begin to create a map to guide you on your learning journey.* *Before we get started, I want you to spend a couple minutes thinking about goals.* Distribute copy of Think-View-Reflect recording page to each student. <table><tr><td colspan="3" align="center">Think – View – Reflect</td></tr><tr><td align="center">Think</td><td align="center">View</td><td align="center">Reflect</td></tr><tr><td>1. What are *goals*? 2. What are *learning goals*?</td><td>Think about how what you hear in the video connects with your own ideas about goals.</td><td>1. What is a goal you've had for yourself in the past? 2. How did you make progress toward the goal? 3. How did you know when you reached the goal?</td></tr><tr><td></td><td></td><td></td></tr></table> **<u>Think:</u>** *Take two minutes to think about the following questions:* 1. **What are goals?** 2. **What are learning goals?** Invite students to share the ideas they have about goals and learning goals prior to watching the video. *Next, we are going to view a short video about goals. As you watch, think about how what you hear in the video connects to your own ideas about goals.*

View: View a short video (2:33) featuring kids explaining their goals: https://www.youtube.com/watch?v=XGd0gq5Fgjc

Today, we are going to spend time thinking about the learning goals we have for ourselves this month (and beyond).

Reflect:
Now, let's spend a bit of time thinking of goals we have set for ourselves in the past. For example, one time I (<u>enter personal example here</u>*).*

Invite students to reflect on the following questions. Then, either in dyads or as whole class, share responses together.

1. What is a goal you had for yourself in the past?
2. How did you make progress toward the goal?
3. How did you know when you reached the goal?

Part II: Identifying Learning Goals

The next segments of this lesson can move in one of two directions:
1. Identifying a learning goal for passion project,
2. Identifying a learning goal for standards-based learning

Learning Goal for Passion Project
It is often useful to introduce passion project goals by sharing examples of others' passion projects to serve as a catalyst for student thinking. This can be accomplished by inviting former students to share a bit about a passion project they completed the past year or by creating a video that features students sharing a bit about their passion project.

Learning Goal for Standards-Based Learning

It is often useful to introduce the standards-based version of goal-setting within differentiated small groups (i.e. guided reading groups, guided math groups). This enables you to work with a small group to complete the first several steps of the template. Then, you can release them to complete the rest working in dyads or with the entire small group. A sample standards-based template can be found in Appendix A.

Decide which path you plan to follow and model with the corresponding "Sample Learning Goal Template" found in Appendix A. The directions below feature both approaches.

An important part of the learning process is identifying what one's learning goal is. In other words: What is it you need to or want to learn? At school, there are usually standards, benchmarks, or progressions to guide this. In sports, your coach may help you identify the goal. Other times, your goal may be related to a hobby or passion of yours and the goal may come from watching others who engage in the hobby.

Today, we are going to work on identifying a learning goal you have for yourself that you want to or need to work toward throughout the weeks ahead.

Task 1: Identifying a Learning Goal

Task: Identify a learning goal you have this month.

What is something you want to or need to know? Record it in the top portion of this template. For example...

(Follow Sample Templates in Appendix A or create your own sample to work from.)

Reminder: Decide in advance if students will use the template to work toward a standards-based goal or a passion project goal. Then, guide them accordingly.

Part III: Mapping Toward a Learning Goal

No matter where a goal comes from, being able to identify a goal is not enough. It is also necessary to think about where you are in relation to the goal, how you will close the gap between what you already know (or are able to do) and what the goal requires you to know (or be able to do), and how you will know when you've met the goal.

This is how you set yourself up to meet the goal (and where the idea of goal-setting comes from!) If the gap between where you are and where you want to be is too large, it probably isn't a very realistic goal for the next month, but that doesn't mean it isn't a goal worth working toward. You would need to break it down into smaller phases – or pit stops – along the way.

This can seem a bit complicated. But it doesn't have to be. I'd like to introduce you to a tool you can use to help you manage your journey toward a learning goal.

This tool is designed to help you map a journey toward a learning goal. We will call it a Learning Goal Template. Let's take a look at an example.

Learning Goal for Passion Project

Project the Learning Goal Template so that all students can see it. Guide students through a sample version using a learning goal you have for yourself. It would likely be helpful to create this as an anchor chart they can refer to as they complete their own work. An example of a completed template is included within the appendix. This can be copied and distributed to students as extra support if needed.

Sample Learning Goal Template for Passion Project:

A learning goal I have for myself this month is:	
I want to learn how to program Lego Spike to move.	
Where am I now? *What can I already do that is related to this goal?*	I can build a robot out of the Lego set. I just don't know how to get the robot to do anything.
Where am I going? *What will I need to learn or practice next in order to reach this goal?*	I need to learn how to program the robot. I think I can use Scratch to program it, but I don't know how.

(continued on the next page)

How am I going to get there? *What is my __action plan__? What steps will I take to reach this goal?*	1. I need to meet with an expert to have them help me figure out Scratch programming. 2. I need to read the directions to see if I can figure it out. 3. I need to try it. 4. I need to learn from my mistakes.
Which <u>learner qualities</u> will be important on this learning journey? Why?	1. Be Determined 2. Reflect I will need to be determined to get the robot to move. It probably won't work right the first time and I need to stick with it. I will need to reflect each time I try so I can figure out what worked and what didn't. That should help me do better with each try.
How will I know I have reached my goal?	I will know I have reached my goal when the robot can move using a program that I wrote.
The evidence I will use to show my learning is…	1. A video of my robot following the program I wrote 2. A screenshot of the program I wrote that makes the robot move 3. Videos of each attempt 4. Screenshots of each program I try 5. A reflection that explains what I figured out from each attempt or tells if I am just STUCK!

Signed: *Sample Student*

Learning Goal for Standards-Based Learning

It is often useful to introduce the standards-based version of goal-setting within differentiated small groups (i.e. guided reading groups, guided math groups). This enables you to work with a small group to complete the first several steps of the template. Then, you can release them to complete the rest working in dyads or with the entire small group. A sample standards-based template can be found in Appendix A.

<u>Sample Learning Goal Template for Standards-Based Learning</u>:

A learning goal I have for myself this month is:	
RF.2.4.A Read grade-level text orally with accuracy, appropriate rate, and expression on successive readings. Learning Goal: "I can read with accuracy, fluency, and expression."	
Where am I now? *What can I already do that is related to this goal?*	I can use different voices for characters. I can accurately read almost all of the words. I can stop at punctuation usually, but not all of the time. This is what I need to improve on!
Where am I going? *What will I need to learn or practice next in order to reach this goal?*	I need to learn to stop at punctuation all of the time. I need to learn to listen to the punctuation and change my voice to show I can hear it. If it's an exclamation point, be excited. If it's a question mark, sound like I'm asking. If it's a period, just sound regular.

How am I going to get there? *What is my __action plan__? What steps will I take to reach this goal?*	Practice reading books. When I'm reading, I will: 1. Actually stop at punctuation. 2. Change my voice for characters 3. Change my voice for punctuation 4. Ask for help if I can't seem to get it.
Which __learner qualities__ will be important on this learning journey? Why?	Be Determined Be Self-Aware
How will I know I have reached my goal?	When I read a book a couple times and I can read the words accurately, fluently, with expression, and pay attention to all of the punctuation
The evidence I will use to show my learning is...	I will ask to read a book to my teacher to show that I have met the goal. I will record myself reading a book to show that I have met the goal. I will read a book to the 1st grade to show that I have met the goal.

Signed: Sample Student

Task 2: Mapping Toward a Learning Goal

Task: Use the template to map a learning journey toward your goal.

Work with students to respond to the questions* below (outlined within the goal-setting template):

1. **Where are you now?**
2. **Where are you going?**
3. **How are you going to get there?**
4. **Which learner qualities will be helpful to you on this learning journey?**
5. **How will you know when you have reached your goal?**
6. **What evidence will you use to show your learning?**

*Questions adapted from the work of Hattie & Timperley (2007) and Fisher, Frey & Hattie (2018).

A learning goal I have for myself this month is:	
Where am I now? *What can I already do that is related to this goal?*	
Where am I going? *What will I need to learn or practice next in order to reach this goal?*	

How am I going to get there? *What is my action plan? What steps will I take to reach this goal?*	
Which learner qualities will be important on this learning journey? Why?	
How will I know I have reached my goal?	
The evidence I will use to show my learning is...	
Signed:	

Closure

Setting goals helps us gain a clear understanding of where we are going with regard to a specific skill or task. Sometimes that goal might be in school other times it might be at home, on a sports team, or some other part of your life.

Creating a learning map for the goal you have helps ensure you reach the goal.

Thinking about which learner qualities you will need and how you will know when you've reached the goal activates your brain to support you as you navigate the journey toward your goal.

Assessment	Collect students' goal-writing work. Provide each student with constructive feedback on the completed template.

Special Note	1. Following Lesson 7 students will need time to work toward the goals they've mapped, keeping track of their progress using a learning log. There are a variety of learning log templates available online. It also works well use electronic logs (i.e. Google Docs, SeeSaw, Kidblog.) A sample learning log template can be found in Appendix A.
	2. It typically works best if students have at least two blocks of time to work toward their learning goal before engaging in Lesson 9.

Lesson 8: Learning Tools	
Overview	This lesson introduces students to the concept of learning tools; strategies that can be used to promote learning.
Learning Intention	I understand what learning is and how to use my awareness of the learning process to grow my knowledge and abilities.
Success Criteria	❑ I can reflect on a time I learned something new and explain how I knew I was learning. ❑ I can describe the difference between learning and practicing. ❑ I can respond to the question "Where does learning come from?" based on my own experience and storybook characters' experiences. ❑ I can use the Learning Pit to map and describe my journey as a learner. ❑ I can use the Learning Pit to map and describe a storybook character's journey as a learner. ❑ I can identify qualities of a strong learner. ❑ I can use a progression to grow learner qualities. ❑ I can list learning goals I have this _____ (enter time duration here, i.e. week, month, quarter, trimester, semester). ❑ I can use the learning goal template to develop a plan to help me reach the learning goal I have identified. ❑ *I can identify a learning tool, explain its purpose, and describe how to use it.* ❑ *I can select and use learning tools as part of a learning journey.* ❑ I can participate in a Learning Talk to provide helpful feedback to another learner. ❑ I can use feedback from a Learning Talk to advance my progress toward a learning goal. ❑ I can use the progress monitoring template to assess my progress toward a learning goal.
Essential Questions	1. What is learning? 2. How do I know when I'm learning? 3. What makes a strong learner? 4. How do I plan and monitor a learning journey?
Materials	All: ❑ Learning Tools Think-Write-Share Template (1 per student) ❑ Learning Tool Template (or Learning Tool Cards) ❑ Hammer ❑ Potato Peeler (continued on the next page)

	K-1: ❑ Copy of the book "Mrs. Wishy Washy" ❑ Farm Workmat (1 per student) ❑ Full copy of Sample K – 1 content-based lesson plan (Appendix B) **2-3:** ❑ Watch, Write, Wonder recording page (1 per student) ❑ Small tanks ❑ Tadpoles (1 per small group for ½ of class) ❑ Frogs (1 per small group for ½ of class) ❑ Full copy of sample grades 2– 3 content-based lesson plan (Appendix B) **4-6:** ❑ Natural Resources Jigsaw Task Card (1 per student) ❑ Nature Resources Jigsaw Poster Requirements (1 per student) ❑ Nature Resources Jigsaw Exchange of Expertise (1 per student) ❑ "Our Natural Resources" by Jennifer Prior (available on Epic books) ❑ Full copy of grades 4 – 6 content-based lesson plan (Appendix B)
Instructional Strategies	• Think-Write-Share • Cognitive conflict • Think & Draw (K – 2) • Watch, Write, Wonder (3 – 5) • Jigsaw (6 – 8) • Learning Wall (Audit Trail)
Instructional Plan	**Introduction: What is a learning tool?** *Another important part of planning a learning journey is thinking about which tools you have available – or will need to use – during the journey.* *To begin, let's think about what learning tools are. Take a moment to reflect on that idea:* **What is a learning tool?** *Write or draw what first comes to mind when you think about the idea of a learning tool.*

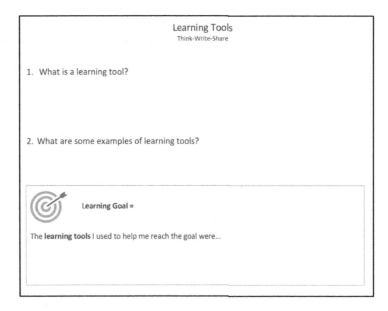

Note: It is very common to students – particularly primary grade students – to think of things like pencils, scissors, markers, and glue. Accept these ideas without evaluation. Then, create a bit of cognitive dissonance by posing a question like:

> *How did the pencil help you learn how to add? spell?*

Aha, it sounds like the pencil helped you show *your thinking and* show *your learning.*

*What helped you **learn**? How did your brain move from not knowing how to add with regrouping to being able to add with regrouping? What learning tools – or learning strategies – helped you accomplish this? Take another minute and write or draw a response to that question:*

> *What learning tools – or learning strategies – helped you learn how to __(enter recent learning topic/concept here)__?*

Record your response in the rectangle at the bottom of your recording page.

This question typically helps transition students' thinking away from school supplies and learning tools that <u>document</u> thinking toward tools – or strategies – that <u>foster</u> or <u>stretch thinking</u>. For example, responses to "***What learning tools – or learning strategies – helped you learn how to*** *add with regrouping*?" might include:

1. **Using math tools:**
   - ➤ **Tens frames** – "I could tell when the frame was full that I had made a ten. Then I move it to the tens place."
   - ➤ **Base 10 Blocks** – "I count out the ones and then, if I get to ten, I trade for a tens rod."
2. **Drawing a picture** – "I draw ones blocks and circle when I get to a group of ten."
3. **Watching someone else** – "We watched a video that showed me how to do it. Then I tried it and I could do what the video showed."
4. **Practice** –" I didn't get it at first. But I practiced a LOT and now I can do it."

There are many learning tools (or strategies for learning) that are available to us as learners. And, it's really helpful when we have a clear sense of what the purpose and value of a specific learning tool is.

This is very similar to when you're working with cooking tools or construction tools. It's important to know <u>how to use</u> to a tool. It's also important to know <u>when to use</u> the tool. For example,

- *You wouldn't want to use a hammer to paint the walls in your living room, you would use a (paint brush).*

- *You wouldn't want to use a potato peeler to spread peanut butter on your sandwich, you would use a (knife or spoon).*

Most tools are really good for certain tasks and not so great for others. It's important to know what a tool is, how to use it, and when it's the best tool for a job.

Throughout the year, we will work to add to your learner's toolbox. This will help you have more tools available as part of your learning journeys.

Part II: Explicit Instruction on Learning Tool of Focus

Today we are going to learn about a tool called:
(lesson differentiation begins here)

Grades K – 1: <u>Think & Draw</u>
Grades 2 – 3: <u>Watch, Write, Wonder</u>
Grades 4 – 6: <u>Jigsaw</u>

	See Appendix B for a full copy of the lesson plans to guide introduction of the "Think & Draw," "Watch, Write, Wonder," and "Jigsaw" learning tools.
	Closure The closure for each Learning Tool lesson can be found within the differentiated lessons in Appendix B.
Assessment	Have students rate their understanding of the learning tool of focus using the rubric below each lesson plan in Appendix B.
Special Note	For a list of thinking/learning strategies consult: • *Tools to Ignite Curiosity* by Goodwin, et al. • *The Power of Making Thinking Visible* by Ron Ritchart and Mark Church. • *The Writing Strategies Book* by Jennifer Serravallo • *The Reading Strategies Book* by Jennifer Serravallo

Lesson 9: Learning Talks	
Overview	This lesson guides students through the process of providing constructive feedback on one another's learning goals. The lesson is meant to be facilitated over at least two class periods' worth of learning time.
Learning Intention	I understand what learning is and how to use my awareness of the learning process to grow my knowledge and abilities.
Success Criteria	❑ I can reflect on a time I learned something new and explain how I knew I was learning. ❑ I can describe the difference between learning and practicing. ❑ I can respond to the question "Where does learning come from?" based on my own experience and storybook characters' experiences. ❑ I can use the Learning Pit to map and describe my journey as a learner. ❑ I can use the Learning Pit to map and describe a storybook character's journey as a learner. ❑ I can identify qualities of a strong learner. ❑ I can use a progression to grow learner qualities. ❑ I can list learning goals I have this _____ (enter time duration here, i.e. week, month, quarter, trimester, semester). ❑ I can use the learning goal template to develop a plan to help me reach the learning goal I have identified. ❑ I can identify a learning tool, explain its purpose, and describe how to use it. ❑ I can select and use learning tools as part of a learning journey. ❑ *I can participate in a Learning Talk to provide helpful feedback to another learner.* ❑ *I can use feedback from a Learning Talk to advance my progress toward a learning goal.* ❑ I can use the progress monitoring template to assess my progress toward a learning goal.
Essential Questions	1. What is learning? 2. How do I know when I'm learning? 3. What makes a strong learner? 4. How do I plan and monitor a learning journey?
Materials	❑ Think-Write-Share recording page ❑ Role Cards (1 set per group) ❑ Learning Talk Protocol Presenter Guide (1 per presenter) ❑ Learning Talk Protocol Reviewer Guide (1 per reviewer)

Instructional Strategies	• Think-Write-Share • Fishbowl • Groupwork • Self-Reflection • Feedback
Instructional Plan	**Introduction** *A valuable tool we have for any learning journey we take is a tool called* **feedback**. *Before we dive in, take five minutes to think about the following questions:* Use a think-write-share strategy to promote student engagement with the reflection.

The Nature and Purpose of Feedback
Think-Write-Share

1. What is feedback?

2. When have you received feedback?

3. When is feedback helpful to you?

4. When is feedback not helpful to you?

5. Describe the most valuable kind of feedback for you as a learner.

7. What do you need feedback to be like in order for it to help you improve your abilities? Give an example if you are able.

After students have had time to reflect and record their ideas on the recording page, facilitate a whole-class discussion with the ideas they have.

Feedback is information about how someone is doing on a journey toward a learning goal. Sometimes you may get feedback on how you are doing as a reader. Other times you may receive feedback on how you are doing as a soccer player, or even how you are doing as a member of your family. Feedback comes in many forms, but not all feedback is equally useful.

Research has found that the most useful feedback responds to three questions for a learner:
1. Where am I going?
2. How am I going?
3. Where to next?

Questions from: Hattie, J., & Timperley, H. (2007).

This week we are going to hold a round of "Learning Talks" to provide one another with valuable feedback on the learning journeys taking place. Together, we will help one another identify what's going well and offer one another support on any of the stuck places we've come up against.

To prepare for the Learning Talks, it is helpful to reflect on the learning you've done so far.

(Project learning talk presenter guide and distribute a copy to every student.)

Today, I want you to take time to prepare for when you are the presenter within a Learning Talk. We will use this form to guide our work. Be prepared to share this with a small team of your classmates tomorrow.

Presenter

❏ My learning goal is....

❏ What I have done so far is...

❏ The learning tools I've used are...

❏ A mistake I made that was useful was...

❏ One place I'm really stuck is...

❏ What questions or suggestions do you have?

...Thank you for your feedback!

Note: It may be helpful to model completion of the template. Emphasize what a complete response to each question should look like/sound like. Encourage students to be specific so that their peers can gain a clear sense of what they've done so far, what tools have been useful, and which stuck places they've come up against.

Application: Learning Talks Fishbowl

Yesterday you took time to reflect on the learning you've done so far. You used this recording page to prepare for Learning Talks today. (Project Presenter guide on screen.)

Today, we are going to divide into groups of three. When it is your turn to present, you will use the completed Presenter page to share your learning journey (thus far) with the classmates in your group.

When you are a reviewer (listener) in the group, your job will be to record ideas on the Reviewer recording page so you can provide the presenter with helpful feedback to guide his/her learning.

Peer Reviewer #1
Reviewer Name:
❑ An area of strength I notice is...
❑ An area for growth might be...
❑ One learning tool that might be useful is...
❑ One thing you could try to help with the stuck place is...
❑ Questions I have are...
...Thank you for sharing your learning journey!

In order to be certain we understand how this will work, I've asked three of you to model this process for us. We will use the "Fishbowl Strategy" to enable everyone to reflect on what makes a Learning Talk work well and what would make a Learning Talk not as useful.

(Guide students through a sample Learning Talk, pausing to process as a group.)

Note: An alternative to a "live" fishbowl would be to video-record a triad participating in a Learning Talk. Often, it is particularly effective to video-record three teachers playing the role of students participating in a Learning Talk. This option is highly engaging for students *and* you can purposefully role play effective and/or ineffective attributes of a Learning Talk. For example, one reviewer could keep saying, "You did good" (empty feedback) or a presenter could say, "I used a lot of tools" instead of being specific. As a teacher, this enables you to be deliberate about highlighting the dispositions you hope to see across set of Learning Talks that take place following demonstration of the Learning Talk strategy.

Following the Fishbowl enactment of a Learning Talk (whether video-recorded or live), guide students through the following points to ponder.

Presenter Points to Ponder:
   1. Was it easy to understand the presenter's learning goal? If yes, what helped make it clear? If no, what would have made it clearer?
   2. Was it clear which tools the presenter has used so far? If yes, what made it clear? If no, what would have made it clearer?
   3. Is there anything the Presenter could have done to be more clear about his/her stuck place? If yes, describe.

Note: The "Reviewer Points to Ponder" (listed below) will need to be custom fit to the context of your classroom. The questions that follow are provided as an example.

Reviewer Points to Ponder:
   1. The first reviewer said, "You're doing good" as feedback for an area of strength. Would this be helpful to you as a learner? Why or why not? Is there anything that would help more, or not?

2. The second reviewer said, "One learning tool that might be useful is reading." Is there a way this reviewer could have been more specific? How could s/he have maximized her support of the learner in this area?

Points to emphasize:
1. When offering feedback about a learning tool someone could try, be sure to explain ***why*** you think the tool would be useful.
2. *When offering feedback on a strength, **be specific** about what made something a strength. For example, "An area of strength was the video you made." This feedback can be strengthened by being more specific: "An area of strength was the video you made that showed you working toward your learning goal. This was helpful because it showed that you have figured out how to fold the origami crane."*

(Optional recording pages to document student reflections can be found in Appendix A.)

Learning Talk
Fishbowl Reflection

1. Was the **learning goal** clear?

2. Were the **learning tools** clear?

3. Were the **stuck places** clear?

Notes:

**Learning Talk
Fishbowl Reflection**

<u>Presenter Points to Ponder:</u>

1. Were you able to understand the presenter's **learning goal?**
   - If yes, what helped to make it clear?

   - If no, what would have made it more clear?

2. Was it clear which **learning tools** the presenter has used so far?
   - If yes, what made it clear?

   - If no, what would have made it more clear?

3. Is there anything the presenter could have done to be more clear about his/her **stuck place**?
   - If yes, describe.

Notes:

Task: Learning Talks

When students are clear about the process of participating in a Learning Talk, divide them into groups and instruct them to begin. Remind students to proceed to the next presenter as each cycle of Learning Talks comes to an end.

Closure

In order to make feedback a powerful tool for learning, it is necessary to think very carefully about how you will use the feedback to advance your learning. We are going to end today by practicing that step.

Individual Reflection:
How was the Learning Talk experience valuable to you as a learner?
What feedback will you use improve your learning journey?

Allow time for students to complete closing reflection.
Then, close with the following key points:

Conducting Learning Talks will enable us to support one another in very

	strategic and specific ways as we work toward our collection of learning goals. *Today we conducted a round of Learning Talks with your peers. It might also be useful to hold a Learning Talk with family members, community experts, or others. We will explore these other paths throughout the weeks and months ahead.*
Assessment	**Option 1**: Review recording pages completed as students conduct peer review sessions. Identify areas of strength and areas in need of additional attention. **Option 2**: Video-record Learning Talks and offer each small group specific feedback on strengths and areas for growth with the Learning Talk process.

Lesson 10: Monitoring Learning Progress	
Overview	This lesson challenges students to reflect on the progress they've made toward a specific learning goal and use evidence to support their evaluation of progress.
Learning Intention	I understand what learning is and how to use my awareness of the learning process to grow my knowledge and abilities.
Success Criteria	❑ I can reflect on a time I learned something new and explain how I knew I was learning. ❑ I can describe the difference between learning and practicing. ❑ I can respond to the question "Where does learning come from?" based on my own experience and storybook characters' experiences. ❑ I can use the Learning Pit to map and describe my journey as a learner. ❑ I can use the Learning Pit to map and describe a storybook character's journey as a learner. ❑ I can identify qualities of a strong learner. ❑ I can use a progression to grow learner qualities. ❑ I can list learning goals I have this _____ (enter time duration here, i.e. week, month, quarter, trimester, semester). ❑ I can use the learning goal template to develop a plan to help me reach the learning goal I have identified. ❑ I can identify a learning tool, explain its purpose, and describe how to use it. ❑ I can select and use learning tools as part of a learning journey. ❑ I can participate in a Learning Talk to provide helpful feedback to another learner. ❑ I can use feedback from a Learning Talk to advance my progress toward a learning goal. ❑ ***I can use the progress monitoring template to assess my progress toward a learning goal.***
Essential Questions	1. What is learning? 2. How do I know when I'm learning? 3. What makes a strong learner? 4. How do I plan and monitor a learning journey?
Materials	❑ Goal-setting forms (completed in Lesson 7) ❑ Progress Monitoring Template (1 per student) ❑ Learner quality rubrics ❑ Evidence of learning (See Saw, videos, etc.)
Instructional Strategies	• Point to Ponder • Modeling • Feedback Cycle • Learning Wall (Audit Trail)

Instructional Plan	**Introduction**
	Today's lesson begins with a point to ponder: *How do you know when you're lost on a trip?*

Project the image of someone looking lost alongside the point to ponder: **How do you know when you're lost on a trip?**

Explanations may include:
- You are not where you expected to be.
- You don't see anything you recognize.
- You can't find your place on a map.

Project the second point to ponder:
  ➢ **How do you know when you're lost on a learning journey?** |

Much like when you're on a road trip or hiking a trail, an important part of a learning journey is taking time to stop and assess the progress you've made so far. This enables you to figure out how you're doing, where you may need help or extra support, and what your next steps should be to move you closer to your goal; to close the gap between where you are and where you want to be.

Today we are going to spend time reflecting on the progress you have made toward the learning goals you have identified.

Throughout the next (<u>enter time period here</u>), I will take time to meet with each one of you to hear about your learning goal and the progress you've made thus far. The purpose of the conference will be to learn about your journey and determine what we can do to support continued progress toward your learning goal.

Today, we will prepare for learning conferences by creating a report of your progress to date. We will use two templates to guide this work:
1. *The Learning Goal template you created (<u>enter date here</u>)*
2. *Progress Monitoring Template (which I will share today).*

Review

To get started, I want you to take 5 minutes to review the "Learning Goal Template" you created (<u>enter date here</u>). When you are done with that task, please look through your learning log to prime your thinking about the journey you've been on thus far.

Allow students time to review the Learning Goal templates and Learning Logs.

Task

The next step is to assess the progress you've made thus far. To do this, each of you will complete the Progress Monitoring Template.

Project a copy of the Progress Monitoring Template for all to see. Walk through each question to be sure students are clear on what they are supposed to do.

A two-page template is included in Appendix A to guide this work.

Learning Goal
Progress Monitoring Template

Where am I going?

1. What is my learning goal?

2. What are the success criteria for this goal? (How will I know when I've met the goal?)

How am I going?

3. What have I done related to this goal so far?

4. What do I have as evidence of my learning?

5. Which learner qualities have been most valuable to me on this learning journey so far?

Where to next?

6. What are the next steps for this learning journey?

7. What can I do to support my learning?

8. What can my teacher do to support my learning?

9. What can my peers do to support my learning?

10. What can others do to support my learning? (Identify who the others are.)

If I have completed the learning goal...

11. Where does this learning lead me? What related challenge could I try now that I have met my goal?

*Guiding questions (bold font) from Hattie, J. & Timperley, H. (2007). The power of feedback. *Review of Education Research. 77*, 81 – 112.

Questions include:

1. What is my learning goal?
2. What are the success criteria?
3. What have I done related to this goal so far?
4. What do I have as evidence of my learning?

	5. Which learner qualities have been most valuable to me on this learning journey so far? 6. What are the next steps for this learning journey? 7. What can I do to support my learning? 8. What can my teacher do to support my learning? 9. What can my peers do to support my learning? 10. What can others do to support my learning? And, if learning goal has been met… 11. Where does this learning lead me? What related challenge could I try now that I have met my goal? **Closure** *Identifying goals is a powerful tool for learning, but just naming a goal is not enough. We also have to make sure we monitor the progress we are making toward a learning goal. This helps ensure we stay on track <u>or</u> adjust the original plan if and when it becomes clear a new strategy is necessary.* *Throughout the week(s) ahead I will meet with each of you to discuss the progress monitoring you've completed today. Please keep your progress monitoring and goal-setting templates – along with any other evidence of learning –together so we have the documentation we need for your meeting.*

Assessment	Review students' self-assessments. Provide written, spoken or recorded feedback that addresses Hattie & Timperley's (2007) framework:
	    1. Where am I going?
	    2. How am I going?
	    3. Where to next?
	
	Use the completed templates to guide the student-teacher conferences using the Conferring Protocol (Appendix A).

Lesson 11: Essential Questions Revisited	
Overview	This lesson challenges students to respond to the essential questions again and reflect on how their understanding of learning has evolved since Lesson 1.
Learning Intention	I understand what learning is and how to use my awareness of the learning process to grow my knowledge and abilities.
Success Criteria	❑ I can reflect on a time I learned something new and explain how I knew I was learning. ❑ I can describe the difference between learning and practicing. ❑ I can respond to the question "Where does learning come from?" based on my own experience and storybook characters' experiences. ❑ I can use the Learning Pit to map and describe my journey as a learner. ❑ I can use the Learning Pit to map and describe a storybook character's journey as a learner. ❑ I can identify qualities of a strong learner. ❑ I can use a progression to grow learner qualities. ❑ I can list learning goals I have this _____ (enter time duration here, i.e. week, month, quarter, trimester, semester). ❑ I can use the learning goal template to develop a plan to help me reach the learning goal I have identified. ❑ I can identify a learning tool, explain its purpose, and describe how to use it. ❑ I can select and use learning tools as part of a learning journey. ❑ I can participate in a Learning Talk to provide helpful feedback to another learner. ❑ I can use feedback from a Learning Talk to advance my progress toward a learning goal. ❑ I can use the progress monitoring template to assess my progress toward a learning goal.
Essential Questions	1. What is learning? 2. How do I know when I'm learning? 3. What makes a strong learner? 4. How do I plan and monitor a learning journey?
Instructional Strategies	• Reflection • Compare and Contrast
Instructional Plan	*Now that we've spent time learning about learning, I'd like to take some time to reflect on the knowledge you've gained.* *Several weeks ago, when we began this journey, I asked to reflect on this set of essential questions:* 1. What is learning?

	2. How do I know when I'm learning? 3. What makes a strong learner? 4. How do I plan and monitor a learning journey? *Today, I'm going to ask you to do the same. In just a moment, I'm going to distribute a copy of the essential questions recording page again. Take the next 20 minutes to respond to the questions. I encourage you to use the Learning Wall to prime your thinking and respond as thoroughly as you can.* Distribute copy of the essential questions. When students are done, *Now I'm going to distribute the responses you recorded to this same set of questions on (<u>enter date here</u>). When you receive your original recording page, take a moment to read through the responses you recorded. Then, reflect on these questions:* ➢ *As you compare your responses to the essential questions from (<u>enter date here</u>) to today, what do you believe is the important understanding you've gained from learning about learning? Why?* ➢ *What are you wondering about learning now that you were not wondering at the beginning of our learning about learning journey?* **Closure** *Learning about learning will increase your learning power in school, in sports, in music, and more. We will continue to put your new knowledge to use as we grow you skills and capacities in school – and beyond – throughout the weeks and months ahead.*
Assessment	Compare students responses to the essential questions today to those recorded as part of Lesson 1. Make note of any areas that remain in need of additional work or clarification. Weave these areas for growth into learning journeys taking place within passion projects or the standards-based curriculum.

Afterword

While I was writing this book the world experienced the COVID-19 pandemic. The impact on schooling was immediate and immense. As buses and buildings were pulled offline, students and teachers gathered online. What began as a projected four-week effort to flatten the curve stretched months beyond expectations.

At the time of publication (April 2021), many students are returning to face-to-face instruction. Also resuming, after a year-long hiatus, is a tendency for parents, policymakers, and educators to enact deficit thinking. *"These kids are so far behind." "How will they ever catch up?"*

When I hear the fear of "learning loss" articulated in the news, school newsletters, or parent conversations, I wince. Though I share the concern about our children's learning, I find it counterproductive to focus on what didn't happen throughout the past year rather than celebrating what did.

Learners during the COVID-19 pandemic are likely some of the most resilient and adaptive people we know. The pandemic didn't challenge them to adjust course just one time. In many cases, systems, schedules, and routines were altered multiple times over. Despite these adversities, learners rose to face each day, each Zoom session, each Google Hangout, and each new expectation with whatever amount of grit and grace they could muster up.

As we return to school buildings in 2021 and beyond, let's resist the urge to focus on what children did not learn during the global pandemic. Instead, let's explore what they *did learn* under quarantine. Let's honor the learner qualities students strengthened while away from brick-and-mortar schooling – adaptability, ingenuity, and persistence to name a few – and use those qualities to advance learning in all disciplines. Let's remember just how agile learners of all ages can be, and let's help students realize their own power in setting and achieving learning goals.

As the title of this book states, learning matters. And learning happens even when school doors have to be locked. Let's not let the whispers of what wasn't drown out the resilience of what was.

Here's to powerful learning about learning, and here's to all of the other ambitions our students pursue.

Bibliography

Absolum, M., Flockton, L., Hattie, J., Hipkins, R., & Reid, I. (2009). *Directions for assessment in New Zealand (DANZ): Developing students' assessment capabilities.* Wellington, New Zealand: Ministry of Education.

Absolum, M. (2010). *Clarity in the classroom: Using formative assessment for building learning-focused relationships.* Manitoba, Canada: Portage & Main Press.

Alvarez, A. (2020). *Andres and his Rubik's cube madness.* Herndon, VA: Mascot Books.

Aronson, E. (1978). *The jigsaw classroom.* Beverly Hills, CA: Sage Publications.

ClassDojo. (2019). Retrieved from https://www.classdojo.com/

Claxton, G. (2018). *The learning power approach: Teaching learners to teach themselves.* Thousand Oakes, CA: SAGE.

Cornwall, G. (2017). *Jabari jumps.* Somerville, MA: Candlewick Press.

Costa, A. & Kallick, B. (2014). *Dispositions: Reframing teaching and learning.* Thousand Oaks, California: Corwin.

Dewey, J. (1938). *Experience & education.* NY: Touchstone Press.

Dweck, C. (2000). *Self-theories: Their role in motivation, personality, and development.* NY: Psychology Press.

Frey, N., Fisher, D., & Hattie, J. (2018). Developing "Assessment Capable" Learners. *Educational Leadership. 75*(5), 46 – 51.

Gladwell, M. (2008). *Outliers: The story of success.* NY: Little, Brown, and Company.

Harste, J. & Vasquez, V. (1998). The work we do: Journal as audit trail. *Language arts. 75:* 4, 266 – 276.

Hattie, J. & Timperley, H. (2007). The power of feedback. *Review of Education Research, 77,* 81-112.

Hattie, J. (2009) *Visible learning: A synthesis of over 800 meta-analyses relating to achievement.* London, England: Routledge.

Hattie, J. (2012). *Visible learning for teachers: Maximizing impact on learning.* NY: Routledge.

National Governors Association Center for Best Practices, Council of Chief State School Officers. (2010). Common Core State Standards English Language Arts. Washington

DC: National Governors Association Center for Best Practices, Council of Chief State School Officers.

National Governors Association Center for Best Practices, Council of Chief State School Officers. (2010). Common Core State Standards Mathematics. Washington DC: National Governors Association Center for Best Practices, Council of Chief State School Officers.

NGSS Lead States. (2013). *Next generation science standards: For states, by states*. Washington, DC: The National Academies Press.

Nottingham, J. (2007). Exploring the Learning Pit. *Teaching Thinking and Creativity, 8*:2(23), 64 – 68. Birmingham, UK: Imaginative Minds.

Nottingham, J. (2010). Challenging learning. (1st ed.). Alnwick, Northumberland, UK: JN Publishing.

Nottingham, J. (2017). *The learning challenge: How to guide your students through the learning pit to achieve deeper understanding.* Thousand Oakes, CA: SAGE.

Ritchart, R. & Church, M. (2020). *Making thinking visible: Practices to engage and empower all learners.* Hoboken, NJ: Jossey-Bass.

Vasquez, V. (2003). *Negotiating critical literacies with young children.* Mahwah, NJ: Lawrence Erlbaum Associates.

Vasquez, V. (2008). Constructing an audit trail or 'learning wall'. Retrieved from https://www.academia.edu/2206003/Constructing_an_Audit_Trail.

Vélez-Ibáñez, C.G. & Greenberg, J. (1992). Formation and transformation of funds of knowledge among U.S.-Mexican households. *Anthropology & Education Quarterly, 23*: 4, 313-335.

Vygotsky, L. (1978). *Mind and society.* Cambridge, MA: Harvard University Press.

Wiggins, G. (2012). Seven keys to effective feedback. *Educational Leadership, 70:*1, 10 – 16.

Wiliam, D. (2016). The secret of effective feedback. *Educational Leadership, 73*(7), 10 – 15.

Resources on Learner Qualities/Learner Dispositions:

Claxton, G. (2018). *The learning power approach: Teaching learners to teach themselves.* Thousand Oakes, CA: SAGE.

Costa, A. (2001) Habits of Mind. In Costa, A. (Ed). *Developing minds: A Resources book for teaching thinking.* Alexandria, VA: ASCD.

Costa, A. & Kallick, B. (2014). *Dispositions: Reframing teaching and learning.* Thousand Oaks, California: Corwin.

Lucas, B. & Claxton, G. (2009). *Wider skills for learning: What are they, how can they be cultivated, how could they be measured and why are they important for innovation:* The Center for Real-World Learning, University of Winchester, UK. Retrieved from, www.winchester.ac.uk/realworldlearning

Meier, D. (2011). 5 habits of mind. Retrieved from, https://21centuryschools.wordpress.com/2011/06/28/5-habits-of-mind-debroah-meier/

Perkins, D. N., Jay, E., & Tishman, S. (1993). Beyond abilities: A dispositional theory of thinking. *Merrill-Palmer Quarterly: Journal of Developmental Psychology, 39*(1), 1 – 21. Retrieved from, http://psychnet.apa.org/psycinfo/1993-20281-001

Tough, P. (2012). *How children succeed.* New York, NY: Houghton Mifflin Harcourt.

Resources on Learning Tools or Learning Strategies:

Goodwin, B., Silver, H., Kreisman, S., & Perini, M. (2019) *Tools for igniting curiosity: Classroom-ready techniques for increasing student engagement and inspiring the love of learning.* Silver Strong & Associates; McREL International.

Ritchart, R. & Church, M. 2020). *The Power of Making Thinking Visible.* Hoboken, NJ: Jossey-Bass.

Serravallo, J. (2015). *The reading strategies books: Your everything guide to developing skilled readers.* Portsmouth, NH: Heinemann.

Serravallo, J. (2017). *The writing strategies books: Your everything guide to developing skilled writers.* Portsmouth, NH: Heinemann.

APPENDIX A

STUDENT DOCUMENTS

Electronic copies of these documents are available at https://www.tiplearning.com/free-resources

Name: _____   Date: _____

Learning Reflection Recording Page

Last summer, I learned...	I know I was learning because...

Name: _____   Date: _____

Learning Reflection Recording Page

Last month, I learned...	I know I was learning because...

Name: _____   Date: _____

Learning Reflection Recording Page

Last week, I learned...	I know I was learning because...

©TiP Learning, 2021, Learning Matters, ISBN 978-1-7371091-0-5

Name: _____

Date: _____

Learning Reflection Recording Page

Last year, I learned…	I know I was learning because…

Learning About Learning

1. What is learning?

2. How do I know when I'm learning?

3. What makes a strong learner?

4. How do I plan and monitor a learning journey?

Name: _____   Date: _____

Learning About Learning
Essential Questions

1. What is learning?

2. How do I know when I'm learning?

3. What makes a strong learner?

4. How do I plan and monitor a learning journey?

Name: _____   Date: _____

Where does learning come from?

(Look, Think, Write)

Look at the list.

Think about the question.

Write your response.

Where does learning come from?

 ©TiP Learning, 2021, Learning Matters, ISBN 978-1-7371091-0-5

Name: _____   Date: _____

Learning Goal: _____

Name: _____   Date: _____

Lesson 3 Exit Slip

➢ **Think** about what we learned about learning today.

➢ **Review** the list of essential questions guiding our learning journey.

➢ **Reflect**: Which essential questions did our learning today connect to? Circle each question you believe today's learning responded to.

➢ **Respond**: Explain why you circled the questions you selected.

Essential Questions:

1. What is learning?

2. How do I know when I'm learning?

3. What makes a strong learner?

4. How do I plan and monitor a learning journey?

 ©TiP Learning, 2021, Learning Matters, ISBN 978-1-7371091-0-5

Name: _____

Date: _____

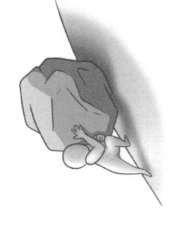

Be Determined

I do not give up when I am faced with a challenge.

©TiP Learning, 2021, Learning Matters, ISBN 978-1-7371091-0-5

Be Determined

"I do not give up when I am faced with a challenge."

Beginning	Developing	Area of Strength
If something is challenging, I usually give up.	If something is challenging, I will try a couple times but then I give up.	I know if I keep trying I will get better at the task.
I will say if something is too hard. I can recognize the challenge.	If someone helps me, I will stick with a task.	If one strategy does not work, I know I can try another.
	If someone helps me, I will try to find a new strategy to work on a challenge.	I keep trying until I find my way through a challenge.

Adapted from: Stonefields School https://www.stonefields.school.nz/

©TiP Learning, 2021, Learning Matters, ISBN 978-1-7371091-0-5

Name: _____

Date: _____

Be Determined

Exit Slip

1. Describe a time you enacted the "Be Determined" learner quality this week. How did being determined help you and your learning?

OR

2. Describe a time that would have benefited from the "Be Determined" learner quality this week. How would the experience have changed if you used the "Be Determined" quality?

©TiP Learning, 2021, Learning Matters, ISBN 978-1-7371091-0-5

Name: _____

Date: _____

Be Determined
Exit Slip

1. Draw a picture that shows a time <u>you used</u> **"Be Determined"** this week.

2. Draw a picture that shows a time **"Be Determined"** <u>would have helped you</u> this week.

1.

2.

Tallest Standing Structure

Your challenge is to build the tallest standing structure you can. You may only use the materials you are given. You will have _____ minutes to build the tower.

You will work as a team. Each team member will have a role. At the end of the time, you and your team will have 5 minutes to identify:
- a strength of your structure
- a strength of your team
- an area of improvement for your structure
- an area of improvement for your team

**Materials Manager**	Responsibility: The materials manager picks up materials from the supply table and returns unused materials when the task is complete.
**Presenter**	Responsibility: The presenter shares the team's structure with the class. The presentation should identify: • a strength of your structure • a strength of your team • an area of improvement for your structure • an area of improvement for your team
**Timer**	Responsibility: The timer watches the clock and makes sure the team is aware of how much time is remaining. The timer gives a 10-minute warning, a 5-minute warning, and a 1-minute warning to his/her teammates.

 ©TiP Learning, 2021, Learning Matters, ISBN 978-1-7371091-0-5

Name: _____ Date: _____

Tallest Standing Structure
Learner Quality Reflection

Think about your team's work on the Tallest Standing Structure task. Based on this task alone, where would you place yourself on the Be Determined progression?

Be Determined

"I do not give up when I am faced with a challenge."

Beginning	Developing	Area of Strength
If something is challenging, I usually give up.	If something is challenging, I will try a couple times but then I give up.	I know if I keep trying I will get better at the task.
I will say if something is too hard. I can recognize the challenge.	If someone helps me, I will stick with a task.	If one strategy does not work, I know I can try another.
	If someone helps me, I will try to find a new strategy to work on a challenge.	I keep trying until I find my way through a challenge.

Adapted from: Stonefields School https://www.stonefields.school.nz/

How did the learner quality "Be Determined" impact your team's progress?

If you tried to build another structure (with the same materials and same amount of time), do you think you could improve your structure or not?

    If yes, describe an improvement you would make.

    If no, explain why you believe you couldn't improve the results.

If you were challenged to complete a different task with your team, what is one way you could grow the "Be Determined" quality within your team?

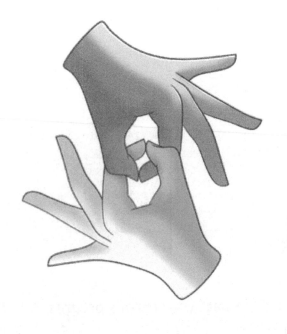

Make Connections

I link prior knowledge and new thinking together to create new understandings.

©TiP Learning, 2021, Learning Matters, ISBN 978-1-7371091-0-5

Make Connections

"I link prior knowledge and new thinking together to create new understandings."

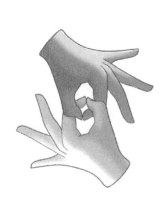

Beginning	Developing	Area of Strength
I do not usually think about how old learning connects with new learning.	I can make simple connections between one idea and another idea.	I work hard to make connections between my knowledge and new learning.
Sometimes I make a simple connection between old learning and new learning.	If someone helps me, I will try to think about how my knowledge connects to new learning.	I work to make connections between ideas even if they do not seem related.
		I make connections between what I am learning in one class and what I am learning in another class.
		I make connections to deepen my understanding.

Adapted from: Stonefields School https://www.stonefields.school.nz/

Name: _____

Date: _____

Make Connections:
What is a neuron?

Source 1

Source 2

 ©TiP Learning, 2021, Learning Matters, ISBN 978-1-7371091-0-5

Name: _____

Date: _____

Think – View – Reflect

Think	View	Reflect
1. What are *goals*? 2. What are *learning goals*?	Think about how what you hear in the video connects with your own ideas about goals.	1. What is a goal you've had for yourself in the past? 2. How did you make progress toward the goal? 3. How did you know when you reached the goal?

Name: _____   Date: _____

A learning goal I have for myself this month is:

Where am I now? *What can I already do that is related to this goal?*	
Where am I going? *What will I need to learn or practice next in order to reach this goal?*	

©TiP Learning, 2021, Learning Matters, ISBN 978-1-7371091-0-5

How am I going to get there? *What is my __action plan__? What steps will I take to reach this goal?*

Which learner qualities will be important on this learning journey? Why?

How will I know I have reached my goal?	The evidence I will use to show my learning is...	

Signed:

 ©TiP Learning, 2021, Learning Matters, ISBN 978-1-7371091-0-5

Name: _Sample Student_   Date: _5/15/21_

A learning goal I have for myself this month is:

I want to learn how to program Lego Spike to move.

Where am I now? *What can I already do that is related to this goal?*	I can build a robot out of the Lego set. I just don't know how to get the robot to do anything.
Where am I going? *What will I need to learn or practice next in order to reach this goal?*	I need to learn how to program the robot. I think I can use Scratch to program it, but I don't know how.

How am I going to get there? *What is my action plan? What steps will I take to reach this goal?*	1. I need to meet with an expert to have them help me figure out Scratch programming. 2. I need to read the directions to see if I can figure it out. 3. I need to try it. 4. I need to learn from my mistakes.
Which learner qualities will be important on this learning journey? Why?	1. Be Determined 2. Reflect I will need to be determined to get the robot to move. It probably won't work right the first time and I need to stick with it. I will need to reflect each time I try so I can figure out what worked and what didn't. That should help me do better with each try.
How will I know I have reached my goal?	I will know I have reached my goal when the robot can move using a program that I wrote.
The evidence I will use to show my learning is…	1. A video of my robot following the program I wrote 2. A screenshot of the program I wrote that makes the robot move 3. Videos of each attempt 4. Screenshots of each program I try 5. A reflection that explains what I figured out from each attempt or tells if I am just STUCK!

Signed: *Sample Student*

 ©TiP Learning, 2021, Learning Matters, ISBN 978-1-7371091-0-5

A learning goal I have for myself this month is:

RF.2.4.A
Read grade-level text orally with accuracy, appropriate rate, and expression on successive readings.

Learning Goal: "I can read with **accuracy, fluency, and expression.**"

Where am I now? *What can I already do that is related to this goal?*	I can use different voices for characters. I can accurately read almost all of the words. I can stop at punctuation usually, but not all of the time. This is what I need to improve on!
Where am I going? *What will I need to learn or practice next in order to reach this goal?*	I need to learn to stop at punctuation all of the time. I need to learn to listen to the punctuation and change my voice to show I can hear it. If it's an exclamation point, be excited. If it's a question mark, sound like I'm asking. If it's a period, just sound regular.

How am I going to get there? *What is my action plan? What steps will I take to reach this goal?*	Practice reading books. When I'm reading, I will: 1. Actually stop at punctuation. 2. Change my voice for characters 3. Change my voice for punctuation 4. Ask for help if I can't seem to get it.
Which learner qualities will be important on this learning journey? Why?	Be Determined Be Self-Aware
How will I know I have reached my goal?	When I read a book a couple times and I can read the words accurately, fluently, with expression, and pay attention to all of the punctuation
The evidence I will use to show my learning is...	I will ask to read a book to my teacher to show that I have met the goal. I will record myself reading a book to show that I have met the goal. I will read a book to the 1st grade to show that I have met the goal.

Signed: *Sample Student*

 ©TiP Learning, 2021, Learning Matters, ISBN 978-1-7371091-0-5

Name: _____

Date: _____

Learning Log

Learning Goal:
Activity: *(Describe what you did <u>today</u> to work toward your learning goal.)*
Select: ☐ Question/Wonder/Ask ☐ Gather Information ☐ Experiment/Try It ☐ Reflect ☐ Other _____
Description of activity:
One thing I did well was:
One thing I can improve on is: b

The **learner quality** I used the most today was:

Questions I have as a result of today's work:

The **next steps** I will take during the next work session are:

Materials I need to round up before the next work session:

©TiP Learning, 2021, Learning Matters, ISBN 978-1-7371091-0-5

Learning Tools
Think-Write-Share

1. What is a learning tool?

2. What are some examples of learning tools?

Learning Goal =

The **learning tools** I used to help me reach the goal were...

The Nature and Purpose of Feedback
Think-Write-Share

1. What is feedback?

2. When have you received feedback?

3. When is feedback helpful to you?

4. When is feedback not helpful to you?

5. Describe the most valuable kind of feedback for you as a learner.

6. What do you need feedback to be like in order for it to help you improve your abilities? Give an example if you are able.

 ©TiP Learning, 2021, Learning Matters, ISBN 978-1-7371091-0-5

Name: _____ Date: _____

**Learning Talk
Fishbowl Reflection**

	YES	NO
1. Was the **learning goal** clear?	☐	☐
2. Were the **learning tools** clear?	☐	☐
3. Were the **stuck places** clear?	☐	☐

Notes:

©TiP Learning, 2021, Learning Matters, ISBN 978-1-7371091-0-5 131

Name: _____ Date: _____

**Learning Talk
Fishbowl Reflection**

Presenter Points to Ponder:

1. Were you able to understand the presenter's **learning goal?**
   - If yes, what helped to make it clear?

   - If no, what would have made it more clear?

2. Was it clear which **learning tools** the presenter has used so far?
   - If yes, what made it clear?

   - If no, what would have made it more clear?

3. Is there anything the presenter could have done to be more clear about his/her **stuck place**?
   - If yes, describe.

Notes:

 ©TiP Learning, 2021, Learning Matters, ISBN 978-1-7371091-0-5

Presenter

- [ ] My learning goal is…
- [ ] What I have done so far is…
- [ ] The learning tools I've used are…
- [ ] A mistake I made that was useful was…
- [ ] One place I'm really stuck is…
- [ ] What questions or suggestions do you have?

- [ ] …Thank you for your feedback!

Peer Reviewer #2

- [ ] An area of strength I notice is…
- [ ] An area for growth might be…
- [ ] One learning tool that might be useful is…
- [ ] One thing you could try to help with the stuck place is…
- [ ] Questions I have are…

- [ ] …Thank you for sharing your learning journey!

Peer Reviewer #1

- [ ] An area of strength I notice is…
- [ ] An area for growth might be…
- [ ] One learning tool that might be useful is…
- [ ] One thing you could try to help with the stuck place is…
- [ ] Questions I have are…

- [ ] …Thank you for sharing your learning journey!

Peer Reviewer #3

- [ ] An area of strength I notice is…
- [ ] An area for growth might be…
- [ ] One learning tool that might be useful is…
- [ ] One thing you could try to help with the stuck place is…
- [ ] Questions I have are…
- [ ] …Thank you for sharing your learning journey!

Presenter
Name:

❑ My learning goal is….

❑ What I have done so far is...

❑ The learning tools I've used are...

❑ A mistake I made that was useful was...

❑ One place I'm really stuck is...

❑ What questions or suggestions do you have?

...Thank you for your feedback!

 ©TiP Learning, 2021, Learning Matters, ISBN 978-1-7371091-0-5

Peer Reviewer #1

Reviewer Name:

Presenter Name:

❑ An area of strength I notice is…

❑ An area for growth might be…

❑ One learning tool that might be useful is…

❑ One thing you could try to help with the stuck place is…

❑ Questions I have are…

…Thank you for sharing your learning journey!

✎ ©TiP Learning, 2021, Learning Matters, ISBN 978-1-7371091-0-5

Peer Reviewer #2

Reviewer Name:

Presenter Name:

❑ An area of strength I notice is...

❑ An area for growth might be...

❑ One learning tool that might be useful is...

❑ One thing you could try to help with the stuck place is...

❑ Questions I have are...

...Thank you for sharing your learning journey!

©TiP Learning, 2021, Learning Matters, ISBN 978-1-7371091-0-5

Peer Reviewer #3

Reviewer Name:

Presenter Name:

❑ An area of strength I notice is...

❑ An area for growth might be...

❑ One learning tool that might be useful is...

❑ One thing you could try to help with the stuck place is...

❑ Questions I have are...

...Thank you for sharing your learning journey!

✎ ©TiP Learning, 2021, Learning Matters, ISBN 978-1-7371091-0-5

Parent Reviewer
Reviewer Name:
Presenter Name:

❑ An area of strength I notice is...

❑ An area for growth might be...

❑ One learning tool that might be useful is...

❑ One thing you could try to help with the stuck place is...

❑ Questions I have are...

...Thank you for sharing your learning journey!

©TiP Learning, 2021, Learning Matters, ISBN 978-1-7371091-0-5

Community Expert Reviewer

Reviewer Name:

Presenter Name:

❑ An area of strength I notice is…

❑ An area for growth might be…

❑ One learning tool that might be useful is…

❑ One thing you could try to help with the stuck place is…

❑ Questions I have are…

…Thank you for sharing your learning journey!

©TiP Learning, 2021, Learning Matters, ISBN 978-1-7371091-0-5 139

Name: _____ Date: _____

Using Feedback to Advance Learning

Think about the feedback you received as part of the Learning Talk you conducted with your classmates.

1. Which feedback do you believe will be the most useful to you as you continue toward your learning goal?

2. How will you use this feedback? Be specific. Provide a step-by-step plan.

3. Are there any questions you have about any of the feedback you received? If yes, list them.

 ©TiP Learning, 2021, Learning Matters, ISBN 978-1-7371091-0-5

Point to Ponder: How do you know when you're lost?

©TiP Learning, 2021, Learning Matters, ISBN 978-1-7371091-0-5

Name: _____ Date: _____

Learning Goal
Progress Monitoring Template

Where am I going?

   1. What is my learning goal?

   2. What are the success criteria for this goal? (How will I know when I've met the goal?)

How am I going?

   3. What have I done related to this goal so far?

   4. What do I have as evidence of my learning?

   5. Which learner qualities have been most valuable to me on this learning journey so far?

©TiP Learning, 2021, Learning Matters, ISBN 978-1-7371091-0-5

Where to next?

6. What are the next steps for this learning journey?

7. What can I do to support my learning?

8. What can my teacher do to support my learning?

9. What can my peers do to support my learning?

10. What can others do to support my learning? (Identify who the others are.)

If I have completed the learning goal...

11. Where does this learning lead me? What related challenge could I try now that I have met my goal?

*Guiding questions (bold font) from Hattie, J. & Timperley, H. (2007). The power of feedback. *Review of Education Research.* 77, 81 – 112.

Conferring Protocol

Where am I going?
1. Tell me about your learning goal.
2. Tell me about the success criteria for this goal. How will you know when you've met the goal?

   Restate what student communicated to ensure a shared understanding of learning intention and success criteria.

How am I going?
1. Tell me about what you have done related to this goal since the last time we met. (Remind student where progress resided at the point of the previous conferring session.)
2. Let's look at some evidence of your progress so far.
   a. What do <u>you</u> have as evidence of your learning?
   b. Let me show you what <u>I</u> have as evidence of your learning (share data from reading log, assessment tool, completed task, etc.)
3. Now, let's talk about what we notice about that evidence.
   a. When I look at [*share specific data source here*], it appears that you are making good progress toward your goal. Or,
   b. When I look at [*share specific data source here*], it appears you have made *some* progress toward your learning goal. Or,
   c. When I look at [*share specific data source here*], it appears that you are not yet making the type of progress we might hope to see.

Where to next?
1. Now, let's talk about what the next steps on this learning journey should be.
   a. Work together to create a list of next steps. (Record ideas on post-it notes. Then, sequence the post-its to create chronology for the steps.)
2. Let's talk about what <u>you can</u> do to support your learning.
3. Let's talk about what <u>I can</u> do to support your learning.
4. Let's talk about what <u>others can</u> do to support your learning.
   a. Peers
   b. Parent(s)
   c. Mentor(s)

*Guiding questions (bold font) from Hattie, J. & Timperley, H. (2007). The power of feedback. *Review of Education Research. 77*, 81 – 112.

 ©TiP Learning, 2021, Learning Matters, ISBN 978-1-7371091-0-5

APPENDIX B

LEARNING TOOL LESSON PLANS & SUPPLEMENTARY MATERIALS

(Differentiated K – 1, 2 – 3, 4 – 6)

145

	Learning Tools Sample Lesson Grades K -1 "Think & Draw"
Overview	This lesson introduces students to the "Think & Draw" learning tool.
Academic Standard(s)	**Common Core Mathematics (U.S.)** **1.OA *Represent and solve problems involving addition and subtraction.*** 1. Use addition and subtraction within 20 to solve word problems involving situations of adding to, taking from, putting together, taking apart, and comparing, with unknowns in all positions, e.g., by using objects, drawings, and equations with a symbol for the unknown number to represent the problem. 2. Solve word problems that call for addition of three whole numbers whose sum is less than or equal to 20, e.g., by using objects, drawings, and equations with a symbol for the unknown number to represent the problem.
Content Objectives	❑ I can use the "Think & Draw" learning tool to solve a mathematical challenge. ❑ I can explain my solution to my classmates.
Language Objectives	❑ I can **use pictures and numbers** to *solve* a mathematical challenge. ❑ I can *tell* others about the *strategy* I used to solve the mathematical challenge.
Academic Language	❑ Think & Draw ❑ learning tool ❑ strategy ❑ using pictures ❑ using numbers ❑ altogether
Materials	❑ Copy of the book "Mrs. Wishy Washy" by Joy Cowley ❑ Farm Workmat (1 per student) ❑ Mud Challenge Rubric (1 per student) ❑ Full copy of lesson plan (Appendix B)
Instructional Strategies	➢ Think & Draw ➢ Integrating Math and Children's Literature ➢ Shared Reading

Instructional Plan	*Today we are going to learn about a tool called "Think & Draw." This tool is helpful when you need to solve a problem that is too tricky for your brain to "just know."*
	Getting Ready:
	I. Introduce Story II. Read Story III. Read mathematical challenge
	Good Morning Mathematicians, I have a story to share with you today. The story is called <u>Mrs. Wishy Washy</u>*. I'm going to read it through one time. Then I'm going to read it again and have you help me read the story. Are you ready?*
	Read *Mrs. Wishy Washy* two times. Invite students to assist with the reading of "Wishy Washy Wishy Washy" on the second read.
	Today, I want you to imagine that you live on a farm. And, on your farm, there are: ❑ *5 ducks* ❑ *3 picks* ❑ *2 cows*
	Just like in the story, your farm animals keep playing in the mud. So, you decide that you want to buy them some mud-boots so they won't track mud all over the inside of the barn.
	How many boots would you need to order?
	Task:
	How many boots will you need to order? *Do you think you can figure it out?* *You want all of the animals to have one boot on each foot.*
	<u>Check for Understanding & Introduce Learning Tool:</u> **Think & Draw**
	Ok, this is where we are going to try out the "Think & Draw" learning tool.
	First, let's make sure we understand what the problem is. <u>(enter name)</u>, will you please tell us what the mathematical challenge is?

Let's try the "Think & Draw" strategy:
If there was 1 duck that lived on your farm, how many boots would you need to order?

(draw a single duck with two legs on the board)

And let's say that a pig moved onto the farm too. So now there is 1 duck and 1 pig. How many boots would you need to order?

(draw a single pig with four legs next to the duck)

Ok, it seems like you understand the mud boot challenge.

Introduce Materials

I'm going to give you each a workmat to show your powerful thinking. Your job will be to use the "Think & Draw" strategy to help you figure out how many boots you will need to order for the animals on the farm.

(show students their workmats)

I will need _____ boots for the ducks.
I will need _____ boots for the pigs.
I will need _____ boots for the cows.

That means I will need to order _____ boots altogether.

Distribute workmats and allow students approximately 10 – 15 minutes of work time. As the students are working, move around the room and pose "questioning for thinking" prompts to foster the development of logical thinking.

Questioning for Thinking Prompts:
- Tell me about what you're doing.
- Do you notice a pattern, or not?
- Can you show that using a picture, or not?
- Can you show that using numbers, or not?
- How is the *Think & Draw* strategy working?
- Is there another way you could keep track of your work, or not?

	Discourse ("Mathematical Talk"): Invite students to share their workmats and tell about how the ***Think & Draw*** tool helped them solve the mud boot challenge. ***Ok mathematicians, it's time to share the work we did*** • ***What did you do to solve the mud boot challenge? What <u>learning tool</u> did you use?*** • ***How many boots will you need to order for the ducks? How do you know?*** • ***How many boots will you need to order for the pigs? How do you know?*** • ***How many boots will you need to order for the cows? How do you know?*** • ***How many boots should you order <u>altogether</u>?*** <u>**With five minutes remaining in class,**</u> Have students turn to an elbow-partner and complete the following sentence frames: I found that I will need _____ boots ***<u>altogether</u>***. The ***<u>learning strategy</u>*** I used was _____.
Assessment	Review each child's mud book challenge work using the rubric on the following page.

Think & Draw Rubric

	Did Not Meet	Partially Met	Met
Works independently to solve the mud boot challenge	Student could not work independently to develop a solution to the mud boot challenge.	Student worked on a solution to the mud boot challenge but needed assistance from others.	Student worked independently to generate a solution to the mud boot challenge.
Records work at a transitional (pictures *and* numbers) level.	Student could not record his/her work using pictures and numbers.	Student recorded his/her work using pictures OR numbers (but not both).	Student recorded his/her work using pictures AND numbers.
Shares his/her work with others	Student was not able/willing to share his/her work with others.	Student shared his/her work with the class but needed assistance from the teacher to do so.	Student was able to share his/her work with the class in a self-directed manner.

©TiP Learning, 2021, Learning Matters, ISBN 978-1-7371091-0-5

Name: _____

How many boots will you need for all of the animals on your farm?

There are 5 ducks.
There are 3 pigs.
There are 2 cows.

Use pictures and numbers to show your work.

©TiP Learning, 2021, Learning Matters, ISBN 978-1-7371091-0-5   151

Name: _____

 Mud Boot Challenge

I will need _____ boots for the ducks.

I will need _____ boots for the pigs.

I will need _____ boots for the cows.

I will need to order _____ boots **altogether**.

The strategy I used to figure this out was...

 ©TiP Learning, 2021, Learning Matters, ISBN 978-1-7371091-0-5

Learning Tools **Sample Lesson Grades 2-3** **"Watch, Write, Wonder"**	
Overview	This lesson introduces students to the "Watch, Write, Wonder" learning tool.
Academic Standard(s)	**Next Generation Science Standards (U.S.)** Practice 1: Asking Questions and Defining Problems • Ask questions based on observations to find more information about the natural and/or designed world(s). Practice 4: Analyze and Interpret Data • Record information (observations, thoughts, and ideas). • Use and share pictures, drawings, and/or writings of observations.
Content Objectives	❑ I can use my senses to make observations. ❑ I can use words and pictures to record the observations I make. ❑ I can use what I observe to fuel curiosity and ask questions.
Language Objectives	❑ I can **record descriptions** of my **observations**. ❑ I can use my observations and descriptions to **generate questions.**
Academic Language	❑ Watch ❑ Observe ❑ Notice ❑ Describe ❑ Question ❑ Wonder
Materials	❑ Watch, Write, Wonder recording page (1 per student) ❑ Small tanks (1 per small group) ❑ Tadpoles* (1 per small group for ½ of class) ❑ Frogs* (1 per small group for ½ of class) *Tadpoles and frogs can be ordered from www.carolina.com
Instructional Strategies	➢ Watch, Write, Wonder
Instructional Plan	**Getting Ready** *The learning tool we are going to focus on today is called "**Watch, Write, Wonder.**" This tool belongs to the Questioning family of learning tools. It helps fuel curiosity.* *Sometimes we may know a topic we are interested in learning more about, but we aren't exactly sure what the learning goal will be or*

what our investigation question is. The "Watch, Write, Wonder" tool helps us generate questions we might choose to follow.

Let's try it: This month we are going to begin a learning journey focused on development. How do plants develop from seeds into plants? How do tadpoles develop into a frog? How do caterpillars turn into butterflies?

When you get back to your desk, you will find a tank with a creature in it. For the first two minutes I want you to watch the creature. Don't worry about writing or drawing during these two minutes. When that time is up, I will let you know. Then, I will say, "It's time to spend some time writing about what you saw." You are welcome to use words and pictures to record your observations.

Finally, I will ask you to take a few minutes to think of questions you have based on what you saw and what you wrote. (Point to the first two icons on the recording page as you explain this. This helps connect the oral instructions to the visual cues.)

Distribute Watch, Write, Wonder recording pages (Appendix B).

Task

Prompt students following the plan described above.

When students have completed one cycle of Watch, Write, Wonder, prompt them again:

"Now, let's try it again. Take another minute to watch the creature. I challenge you to notice at least one thing you haven't already recorded.

Make your observation and write about it using words and pictures. Then see if that raises any additional wonders or questions for you."

When time is up, gather students as a whole group.

Discourse

Tell me about what you noticed.

Record students' observations on chart paper.

	Now, tell me how watching and writing about the tadpoles and frogs have fueled your curiosity. What are you wondering?
	Record questions on chart paper.
	Take a moment to think about the questions we have listed here. Are there any questions or wonder statements about something you observed that you don't see listed here yet? If yes, what are they?
	Learning About Learning:
	Now I want to walk our thinking away from the tadpoles and toward the "Watch, Write, Wonder" learning tool.
	➢ *How did this tool help you grow your Questioning abilities?*
	Sometimes if we are not sure what we want to know about a new topic or idea, we can use the Watch, Write, Wonder tool to help us notice things we are curious about and develop questions or wonderings we want to investigate.
	➢ *Do you think you could use this tool on your own sometime, or not?*
Assessment	Review each child's "Watch, Write, Wonder" recording page and gauge their progress toward content objectives using the rubric on the following page.

Watch, Write, Wonder Rubric

	Did Not Meet	Partially Met	Met
Watch **I can use my senses to make observations about tadpoles and/or frogs.**	I did not use my senses to make observations.	With help, I could use my senses to make observations about tadpoles and/or frogs.	I used my senses to make observations about tadpoles and/or frogs.
Write **I can use words and pictures to record the observations I make.**	I did not use words and pictures to record the observations I made.	With help, I can use words and pictures to record the observations I made.	I used words and pictures to record the observations I made.
Wonder **I can use what I observe to fuel curiosity and ask questions.**	I cannot yet use what I observed to ask a question about tadpoles and/or frogs.	With help, I used my observations to ask a question about tadpoles and/or frogs.	I used my observations to generate questions about frogs and/or tadpoles.

©TiP Learning, 2021, Learning Matters, ISBN 978-1-7371091-0-5

Watch, Write, Wonder

1.

2.

3.

4.

©TiP Learning, 2021, Learning Matters, ISBN 978-1-7371091-0-5   157

Learning Tools Sample Lesson Grades 4 – 6 "Jigsaw"	
Overview	This is an introductory lesson about natural resources that also introduces students to the "Jigsaw" learning tool:
Academic Standard(s)	**Common Core English Language Arts** (U.S.) W.4.2. Write informative/explanatory texts to examine a topic and convey ideas and information clearly. **Next Generation Science Standards** (U.S.) 4-ESS3-1. Obtain and combine information to describe that energy and fuels are derived from natural resources and their uses affect the environment. ESS3.A: Natural Resources Energy and fuels that humans use are derived from natural resources, and their use affects the environment in multiple ways. Some resources are renewable over time, and others are not.
Content Objectives	❏ I can use the Jigsaw strategy to build background knowledge about natural resources. ❏ I can use the knowledge I gain from the Natural Resources Jigsaw to write two paragraphs that explain: 1. What natural resources are and why they are important, and 2. How the use of natural resources affects the environment (including the different the between renewable and non-renewable resources).
Language Objectives	❏ I can **teach** my peers about natural resources. ❏ I can **write** a paragraph about natural resources.
Academic Language	❏ Natural Resources ❏ Fossil Fuels ❏ Renewable resources ❏ Non-renewable resources ❏ Jigsaw
Materials	❏ Natural Resources Jigsaw Task Card (1 per student) ❏ Nature Resources Jigsaw Poster Requirements (1 per student) ❏ Nature Resources Jigsaw Exchange of Expertise (1 per student) ❏ "Our Natural Resources" by Jennifer Prior (available on Epic books)

Instructional Strategies	➢ Jigsaw
Instructional Plan	*Today, we are going to work to build background knowledge about Natural Resources using a learning tool called "Jigsaw." Jigsaw belongs to the Gathering Information family of learning tools.* *The Jigsaw tool is useful when you want to develop expertise about a topic using a variety of sources, but you want to share the responsibility of learning all of the information.* *Here's how the tool works:* *Each of you will be assigned to a specific section of information about natural resources. To begin, you will read the material you are assigned and take notes that respond to the questions we are trying to build background knowledge around.* **Group 1: Pages 4 - 7** **Group 2: Pages 8 - 13** **Group 3: Pages 14 - 21** **Group 4: Pages 22 - 25** **Group 5: Pages 26 - 29** *Next, you will meet with a small group of students who have read the same material as you. This will be called your "Expert Group." Together, you will become experts about the reading material and question to which you were assigned.* ➢ *It is very important that every member of the Expert Group builds expertise, because each of you will be responsible for teaching others about the background information gained from the section you read.* *Once you have developed expertise within your Expert Group, you will join your Jigsaw group. Jigsaw groups will be made up of 1 expert representing each section of the reading material. In your Jigsaw group, you will take turns teaching one another the background information you gained from the section you read.* *When the Jigsaw groups have completed the exchange of expertise, each of you will be responsible for writing two paragraphs that summarize the information we've learned about natural resources and address the following questions:* *Paragraph 1:*

	❑ What are natural resources? ❑ What are some of Earth's natural resources? ❑ How do we use natural resources? Paragraph 2: ❑ What makes an energy source renewable? non-renewable? ❑ What are some ways that non-renewable natural resources can be conserved? Each paragraph should include: ❑ Topic sentence ❑ Detail sentences ❑ Academic Language ❑ Conclusion Learning About Learning: *Now I want to walk our thinking away from the natural resources and toward the "Jigsaw" learning tool.* ➢ *How did this tool help you grow your Gathering Information abilities?* ➢ *What are the benefits of the Jigsaw learning tool?* ➢ *When would the Jigsaw be a good tool to use?* ➢ *When would the Jigsaw not be as useful?*
Assessment	Review the paragraphs generated by students following the Jigsaw activity centered on natural resources. Gauge their progress toward content objectives using the rubric on pages 126 and 127.
Special Note	The jigsaw strategy was first developed by Elliot Aronson. For background information see Aronson's website: www.jigsaw.org

Natural Resources Jigsaw

Part I: Building Background Knowledge

Directions:
1. Read the material to which you have been assigned.
2. Take notes that respond to the questions below as you read.

Focus Questions:

Group 1: What are natural resources?

Group 2: What are essential resources? Why are they essential?

Group 3: What are hidden natural resources? Provide examples and explain where they come from.

Group 4: What makes a resource renewable? Non-renewable? Provide examples of each.

Group 5: Why is it important to conserve natural resources?

Part II: Meet with Expert Group

Meet with the group of students who have been assigned to the same reading material as you. Prepare a hand-out you will use to teach others in your Jigsaw group about the topic you have read about. The hand-out should include the following information.

1. **Title of section you read**
2. **What the author says about the question of focus**
3. **An illustration that conveys the main idea(s)**
4. **Questions you have as a result of the reading**

Part III: Meet with Jigsaw Group

Return to your Jigsaw group. Each person will take a turn to present the information they've become an expert on. When you are not presenting, you should listen carefully, take notes on the information being shared, and ask questions to clarify your understanding of the information being shared.

Part IV: Show what you know.

Before you leave class:
1. Write two paragraphs that that:
   - Describe what natural resources are.
   - Explain why natural resources are important to us.
   - Explain how the use of natural resources affects our environment.
   - Distinguish between renewable and non-renewable resources.
2. List 3 questions you have about natural resources as a result of the Jigsaw experience.
3. Use the rubric to guide your work.

Natural Resources Jigsaw
Hand-Out Requirements

Title of Source:

Title of Section:

What your source says about the question of focus:

Question of focus: _____

_____

Answer:

Illustration that conveys the main ideas:	Questions you have as result of the reading:

©TiP Learning, 2021, Learning Matters, ISBN 978-1-7371091-0-5

Natural Resources Jigsaw:
Exchange of Expertise

1. What are natural resources?

2. What are essential resources? Why are they essential?

3. Describe what is meant by the phrase "hidden natural resources". Provide some examples of hidden natural resources and explain where they come from.

4. What makes a resource renewable? Non-renewable? Provide examples of each.

5. Why is it important to conserve natural resources?

Natural Resources Jigsaw Rubric

	Area of Focus	Did Not Meet (1)	Partially Met (2)	Met (3)
I can use the Jigsaw strategy to build background knowledge about natural resources.	Reading & Note-Taking	I did not complete the reading portion of the Jigsaw task.	Content written in notes was mostly correct and mostly highlighted the important information from the assigned part of the text.	Content written in notes was correct and highlighted the important information from the assigned part of the text
	Preparing for Teaching (Expert Group)	I did not work as a team player in the expert group to gain information and prepare to teach others.	Most of the time, I worked as a team player in the expert group to gain information and prepare to teach others.	I worked as a team player in the expert group to gain information and prepare to teach others.
	Teaching (Jigsaw Group)	The information I presented to my jigsaw group was not clear or concise.	The information I presented to my jigsaw group was mostly clear and concise.	The information I presented to my jigsaw group was clear and concise.
I can use the knowledge I gain from the Natural Resources Jigsaw to write two paragraphs that respond to the following prompts: ☐ What are natural resources?	Respond to the required prompts.	The paragraphs I wrote do not respond to the required prompts.	The paragraphs I wrote respond to some, but not all, of the required prompts.	The paragraphs I wrote respond to all of the required prompts.
	Include proper elements: ☐ Topic Sentence ☐ Supporting Details	The paragraphs I wrote do not include the required proper elements of a paragraph.	The paragraphs I wrote include some, but not all, of the proper elements of a paragraph.	The paragraphs I wrote include all of the proper elements of a paragraph.

©TiP Learning, 2021, Learning Matters, ISBN 978-1-7371091-0-5

		I cannot yet explain the purpose and value of the Jigsaw learning tool.	I can describe the purpose of the Jigsaw learning tool or the value of the Jigsaw learning tool, but not both.	I can describe the purpose and value of the Jigsaw learning tool.
☐ Why are natural resources important to us? ☐ How does the use of natural resources affect our environment? ☐ What is the difference between renewable and non-renewable resources?	☐ Academic Language ☐ Concluding Sentence			
I can describe the purpose and value of the Jigsaw learning tool.	☐ Purpose ☐ Value			
			Total:	/18

Comments:

©TiP Learning, 2021, Learning Matters, ISBN 978-1-7371091-0-5

Appendix C

Audit Trail (or Learning Wall)

An audit trail is a map of learning that archives the important topics, concepts, and ideas explored throughout a defined period of time (Harste & Vasquez, 2008; Vasquez, 2003;2008). Comprised of text, images, photographs, and/or samples of student work, the audit trail – also referred to as a learning map or learning wall – helps students of all ages keep learning in sight and in mind across the duration of a learning journey .

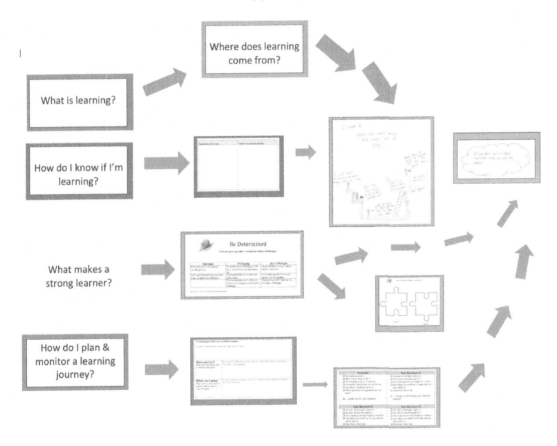

The paragraphs below identify ways to utilize the trail to support student learning across grades K – 8.

Audit trail as assessment

Formatively, an audit trail can be used to help students reflect on the key concepts, topics, or ideas that evolve out of a particular lesson or experience. These become the "big ideas" that are posted on the wall. A second layer of formative assessment involves challenging students to think about connections between and amongst the big ideas. Such connections can be captured through arrows that indicate a relationship between topics. Finally, from a summative perspective, students can be challenged to reflect back on a defined span of learning and use the wall to articulate what they have learned, the connections they've made, questions that have emerged as a result of new knowledge.

Audit trail as engagement

From an engagement perspective, the audit trail helps connect students' experiences to the topics explored during a learning journey. Images of students engaged in tasks or experiences affixed alongside the big ideas and samples of student work literally become the glue (or tape) that hold learning together.

Audit trail as site of collaboration

When an audit trail is displayed on a wall in a classroom or nearby hallway it becomes a site of communication and participation for community members beyond the classroom as well. Other students, school/community members, parents, and siblings can view the trail and gain a clearer sense of the learning that has taken place. The collection of photographs, images, student work samples, and identified links serve as a catalyst for conversation about learning. In this sense, the audit trail becomes a connective force, joining the classroom with the broader community.

Audit trail as reflection tool

In addition to helping students keep learning experiences "in sight and in mind," the audit trail also offers itself as a valuable reflection tool. I often used the trail as an exit slip, providing students with a sheet of paper, asking them to study the wall, and respond to prompts about their learning. See examples below.

Sample Prompts:

- What are 3 important ideas you think we should add to the wall today? Where would they go? What do they connect to? Why?
- Where do you see a connection that is not currently documented on the wall? Describe the connection.
- Which topic or experience would you like to learn more about? Why?
- Which topic or experience is the most challenging for you? What do you think would help you to better understand it?
- How does what we did in math today connect to the nature of science? Use a specific example to make your perspective clear.

Audit trail as archive

Finally, the audit trail serves as an archive of the learning done across the arc of a school year. Students can create a copy of the trail (panoramic photograph or short video) and use it as a reminder of the work they've accomplished together over time.

Made in the USA
Coppell, TX
18 May 2021